Exploring the Catechism

Jane E. Regan

with

Michael P. Horan
Timothy Backous, O.S.B.
Francis Kelly Nemeck, O.M.I.
and
Marie Theresa Coombs

A Liturgical Press Book

THE LITURGICAL PRESS
Collegeville, Minnesota

Cover design by Ann Blattner.
Paper marbling by Margaret VanKempen, O.S.B.

Nihil obstat: Robert C. Harren. *Censor deputatus.*
Imprimatur: Daniel J. Taufen, Administrator, Diocese of St. Cloud, December 16, 1994.

Excerpts from the English translation of the *Catechism of the Catholic Church* for the United States of America Copyright © 1994 by the United States Catholic Conference, Inc. — Libreria Editrice Vaticana. Used with permission. A copy of the *Catechism* may be ordered from The Liturgical Press, Collegeville, Minnesota 56321 (1-800-858-5450).

1   2   3   4   5   6   7   8   9

Library of Congress Cataloging-in-Publication Data

Exploring the Catechism / Jane E. Regan [et al.].
    p.   cm.
    Includes bibliographical references.
    ISBN 0-8146-2152-X
    1. Catholic Church.   Catechismus Ecclesiae Catholicae.
    2. Catholic Church—Catechisms.   3. Catholic Church—Doctrines.
    I. Regan, Jane E.   II. Catholic Church.   Catechismus Ecclesiae
    Catholicae.
    BX1959.5.E87   1995
    238'.2—dc20   94-43318
                                                                    CIP

CONTENTS

Foreword   v

Introduction   1

Part I: Setting the Catechism in Context

  I. The Context of Catechesis   7

    1. Catechesis: "Into the Fullness of the Christian Life"   7

  II. The Context of History   23

    2. The Catechism:
       "Inspired by the Great Tradition of Catechisms"   23

    3. Synod of 1985: Toward "a Catechism or
       Compendium of all Catholic Doctrine"   44

Part II: Opening the Catechism

  Overview   63

    4. The Profession of Faith   71
       Michael P. Horan

    5. The Celebration of the Christian Mystery   96
       Jane E. Regan

    6. Life in Christ   119
       Timothy Backous, O.S.B.

    7. Christian Prayer   138
       Francis Kelly Nemeck, O.M.I.,
       and Marie Theresa Coombs, Hermit

Setting Out with a Map   164

Contributors   167

Index   169

FOREWORD

Each person approaches the reading of the *Catechism of the Catholic Church* from his or her own perspective. The questions we bring and the concerns that present themselves as we read the text are shaped by our roles and responsibilities within the life of the Church community. I come to this text as theologian and catechist. As theologian I ask a number of questions: What is in the *Catechism?* What theological perspective is reflected there? What is *not* in the *Catechism* and why is it not there? As catechist and catechetical theorist I ask other questions: Given the text, what are we to do with it? What is the role of the *Catechism* in the catechetical enterprise of the Church? How does our understanding of contemporary catechesis shape our approach to the *Catechism?* These are the questions I bring to a careful and critical reading of the *Catechism.*

In carefully reading the text, the reader is invited to go beyond simply taking in the words. We approach any text on a variety of levels: On one level we follow the narrative of the text, asking questions about the explicit images being presented or the ideas being explored. At a second level we are attempting to enter into the world being set out in the text. Here the focus is not simply on attending to the words of the text but also on understanding the "world" of the text, the world that allows the ideas being presented to have meaning and to be meaningful. A third level involves entering into the text from our own worlds — from the world of the reader. Our own experiences and how we perceive them shape the way we read and interpret the text, i.e., we approach the text with our own pre-understanding, which provides the basis for our understanding the text. Reading between the lines of any text involves moving beyond the question "What does the text say?" to ask "What does the text mean?" and, finally, "What does the text mean for me?"

To read any text authentically, one must place the text within a broader context. For the *Catechism of the Catholic Church,* that context is multi-faceted and includes the history of catechisms and the way they have been used in the past, as well as the understanding of catechesis and the hopes for the future of that pastoral enterprise. In addition, the theological conversations that have shaped the Church's beliefs and practices serve as an important context, particularly the theological discussions that led up to, and flow from, the Second Vatican Council. These various realities contribute to our exploration of what the text means and what it means for us today, and they contribute to our engaging in the enterprise of reading between the lines.

Since the spring of 1993, I have had the opportunity to present numerous day-long workshops to diocesan and parish catechetical and pastoral leaders throughout the Midwest on the nature and role of the *Catechism of the Catholic Church*. I regularly come away from these workshops hopeful for the pastoral life of the Church and energized in my commitment to catechesis. It was in the company of these groups that much of Part I of this book was reworked and thought through again. Workshop participants may well recognize their questions and insights, and I appreciate their comments and encouragement. Whenever I began to question the need for a book such as this one, their positive responses to some of the book's key ideas sustained me.

Also shaping my understanding of the *Catechism* and enhancing my ability to read between the lines of the text are those who have contributed chapters to Part II: Michael Horan, Timothy Backous, Francis Kelly Nemeck, and Marie Theresa Coombs. From reading their essays and taking part in many conversations with these writers and theologians, I have gained new insight into the theology and perspectives that shape the various books of the *Catechism*.

Many people have read parts of this text and have been willing to discuss it with me. Comments and suggestions from friends, students, and colleagues at St. John's University in Collegeville, Minnesota, have strengthened the text. I owe particular thanks to Mimi Bitzan, Michael Horan, Jean Regan, and Patty Weishaar, who read all of Part I and sections of Part II; their long-term support is appreciated.

As we set about the task of reading and reading between the lines of the *Catechism of the Catholic Church*, of examining the teachings and practices it presents for their meaning and meaningfulness to us, we do so with this injunction from the *Catechism* in mind:

> The whole concern of doctrine and its teaching must be directed to the love that never ends. Whether something is proposed for belief, for hope or for action, the love of our Lord must always be made accessible, so that anyone can see that all the works of

perfect Christian virtue spring from love and have no other objective than to arrive at love (CCC 25).

Jane E. Regan
Holy Week 1994

INTRODUCTION

In late fall of 1985, when rumors first began filtering back from the synod in Rome that a universal catechism was being proposed, the reaction was mixed. Some greeted the idea of a catechism with some relief. The catechism was seen as a refuge in difficult times: here we will find the answers to our questions, and the debates that have shaken the Church will be resolved. Others greeted the idea of a catechism with some hesitation. The catechism was seen as a sign of retrenchment: here we will be given the "party line," and the life-giving spirit of inquiry within a pluralistic Church will be silenced. These perspectives mark the two ends of a broad spectrum of attitudes toward a catechism. The proposal in this book is that the more help-ful stance from which to receive the *Catechism of the Catholic Church* (CCC) is not at either end of this spectrum but somewhere in the middle.

In beginning this exploration of the nature and content of *Catechism of the Catholic Church*, it is important to step back for a moment and reflect on one's attitude toward the very idea of a catechism in general as well as the questions or concerns that are brought to the reading of this particular one. Naming the "pre-understandings" — the presumptions, attitudes, concerns, images that the reader brings to a particular text — sets up the possibility of giving the text a more even-handed reading. Exploring the "pre-judgments" allows the reader to recognize the attitudes and perspectives that shape his or her approach to the catechism and to be aware of them while reading the text.

The "pre-understanding" that shapes one's reading of the *Catechism* can be examined through a series of questions. The first are concerned with the immediate reaction to the idea of a universal catechism. The reader can reflect: What was my first reaction when I heard about the proposal for a universal catechism or when I first heard that there was a catechism "in the works"? Did I see this as a generally positive or negative development? Taking time to examine the concerns or hopes

1

behind that response is helpful in clarifying the attitudes that shape the reading of the *Catechism*.

Through a second set of questions, the reader can explore what she or he imagines a catechism to be: What kind of book did I imagine? What past experience with catechisms defines the kind of book I am picturing? How do I imagine using it? *Do* I imagine using it? In a parish setting, what room does the book belong in: the pastor's office, the DRE's office, the principal's office, each classroom in the parish school, the home of each of the catechists?

The final set of questions is a bit harder to explore but is, in fact, the most significant: What is the connection between a catechism and my ecclesiology, my sense of the nature of the Church, of the role the Church plays? What effect does the decision to produce a catechism of the Catholic Church have on my sense of the Church?

In addition to naming the presumptions and attitudes that are brought to a reading of the *Catechism*, reflecting on these questions also helps bring into focus the complexity of the decision to create a catechism. At some level the creation and reception of a catechism for the Catholic Church raises a wide range of issues and questions: What is the nature of the Church? What is the role of the magisterium or teaching office of the Church? What is meant by collegiality within the Church, and how is it expressed? What are the appropriate expressions of authority within the Church? What are the meanings of such terms as "tradition" or "truth"?

And these are just the intra-Church questions, the questions raised when Roman Catholics speak among themselves about a catechism. The decision to prepare a catechism also raises questions concerning the Church's relationship to contemporary culture, not to mention the Roman Catholic Church's relationship to other Christian Churches and to non-Christian believers.

At some level it seems possible to argue that the most heated discussions about the *Catechism* may not be about its content but about the fact of a catechism and the implications of that fact for how the Roman Catholic Church understands itself and how it understands its relationships with others.

This small book does not hope to address the breadth of questions and issues that are integrally related to the publication and reception of the *Catechism of the Catholic Church*. A more modest set of tasks is at hand: To set the conversation about the *Catechism* in the context of catechesis and history and to provide an overview of the four books of the *Catechism* with a particular concern for their pastoral "fit." Addressed primarily to those engaged in catechesis on the parish and diocesan levels, this book provides an entry point for those wishing to explore the nature and content of the *Catechism*.

Part I names and explores the contextual framework within which to interpret and to convey the meaning of the *Catechism*. The first element of that context is contemporary catechesis: What does the *Catechism* contribute to the catechetical enterprise as it comes to expression in the United States as we move into the twenty-first century? This is examined in chapter 1. The second element of the contextual framework is history: this is not the first catechism ever presented. It is helpful to ask, first, about the history of catechisms as they have appeared across the centuries of Christian formation (chapter 2) and then about this particular catechism as it took shape during the course of the Synod of 1985 (chapter 3). From these various perspectives, one is able to draw out some principles for understanding the nature of this text and for studying its content.

With Part II attention turns to the *Catechism of the Catholic Church* itself. This begins with a consideration of the structure of the *Catechism* and provides insights for reading the text that follows from the structure. Each part is then discussed in turn: Part One: "The Profession of Faith" (chapter 4), Part Two: "The Celebration of the Christian Mysteries" (chapter 5), Part Three: "Life in Christ" (chapter 6), and Part Four: "Christian Prayer" (chapter 7). The focus for each chapter is a discussion of the foundational principles and guidelines that shape the reader's understanding of the specific area of Church teaching addressed in the particular book of the *Catechism*—Creed, sacraments, morality, prayer. Each chapter is written with pastoral ministers in mind, supporting them as they critically read the *Catechism* and endeavor to convey its substance within their pastoral setting.

One may be tempted to summarily dismiss the *Catechism of the Catholic Church* as an unhelpful expression of an outdated, centralized, institutional structure or to blindly embrace it as a much-needed voice of uniformity to silence dissension and disagreement. But neither response takes adequately into account the lived faith of the varied people of God gathered within the Roman Catholic Church. It is the ongoing dialogue among the elements of Scripture, tradition, and lived experience that fosters in the individual, and in the community, continual growth in faith. The *Catechism* can enhance this dialogue if it is approached with openness and situated within the broader context of

Church life. At the same time, the dialogue can also enhance the usefulness of such a text in the catechetical enterprise. In these pages we explore the grounding for this approach to the *Catechism of the Catholic Church*.

PART I
Setting the Catechism in Context

I. The Context of Catechesis

CHAPTER 1

Catechesis: "Into the Fullness of the Christian Life"

> Catechesis . . . includes especially the teaching of Christian doc-
> trine, imparted, generally speaking, in an organic and systematic
> way, with a view to initiating the hearers into the fullness of Chris-
> tian life (CCC 5).

Where do we begin this endeavor of reading the *Catechism of the Catholic Church* (CCC)? We might turn first to the text itself and spend time exploring its content and structure. Careful study of the structure of the *Catechism* does provide insights into its interpretation. Or we might consider the context within which this particular text was forged. Finding answers to questions about why it was written, by whom it was written, and to whom it is addressed can also illumine our interpretation of the text. Or, using a wide-angled lens, we can gain an understanding of this catechism by looking at the history of the genre and the role that catechisms have played in the Church's history. As subsequent chapters make evident, each of these three starting points — the *Catechism* itself, the Synod of 1985 from which the call for a catechism arose, and the history of catechisms — provides pieces that are essential to creating a perspective that can lead to a valid and helpful use of this text. But before moving into these discussions, it is necessary to step back and explore the context within which any consideration of a catechism must take place: the pastoral endeavor of catechesis.

Numerous books have been written on the nature of catechesis and the tasks that it addresses, so an exhaustive exploration of this topic is well beyond the scope of the project we are engaged in here. But an examination of the evolution of catechesis over the past century does allow us to set out in broad strokes the essential elements of a description of catechesis. To do this, we begin with a reflection on scenes from a worshiping and catechizing community from the perspective of two different eras.

SCENES FROM TWO GENERATIONS

Preparing children and adults for the celebration of the Church's sacraments has long been an important role in the life of a parish community. Formation for the reception of First Eucharist is one obvious example that comes to mind. One wonders what went through the minds of catechists from the same parish who have had responsibility for this important process as they reflect on their experience the day after First Eucharist. Let us imagine catechists at St. Odo the Good parish, who reflect upon their tasks of Eucharist preparation. But let us imagine them in two generations in the Church's recent history — 1954 and 1994.

THE DAY AFTER FIRST EUCHARIST: 1954

On the day after First Communion in 1954, Sister Joseph Marie thinks back fondly on her class of forty-three second graders. They were a good class: quiet and attentive. Most of the CCD children came to every session, both the regular Wednesday afternoon classes and the special First Communion classes held on Saturday mornings from January through May. She remembers how quickly they learned their prayers, every child taking his or her turn to recite the prayer aloud, thus earning one more gold star for the Prayer Chart. It was evident to Sister Joseph Marie even then that parents put time into helping the children learn those prayers. And they learned the catechism answers so quickly! Another sign that the parents were really behind her as she prepared their children for First Communion.

But of course the parents support her, Sister Joseph Marie reflects. They are good families, most of them, good Catholic families. They go to Mass each Sunday; there are even some altar boys from the families in this group. Some of the parents attend the monthly novenas, and Sister can recall seeing a good number of these families at the annual parish mission earlier in the spring. Many of the fathers are members of the Knights of Columbus or belong to the St. Vincent

DePaul Society — both organizations do such good work for people in need. And most of the mothers belong to the Sodality or to the Rosary Society. Moreover, they are all so thoughtful about taking food to the homes of those who have had a death in the family. And of course they almost all pitch in for the annual festival! Good people, Sister thinks to herself; they'll do anything for you!

Oh, they aren't perfect, that's for sure. There are some families who don't seem to be attentive enough to night prayers and Sunday Mass. Sister worries about them. But she also recognizes that, even when the parents aren't as attentive as they should be, there are usually other relatives — grandparents, often, or aunts and uncles — who set a good example for the children. These relatives are usually more than willing to go out of their way to bring the children to Mass with them and to make sure the children get to catechism instruction. And when there aren't relatives around, the neighbors often step in. Sister recalls that after Mrs. Kennedy gave birth to little Annie, Miss Lopotowski stopped by their home each Sunday to pick up the older three children for Mass and even brought Brian to church on Saturday so that he wouldn't get behind in his First Communion classes.

Yes, Sister Joseph Marie recognizes that there are so many other people and events in these children's lives that make her job of teaching them the catechism so much easier!

THE DAY AFTER FIRST EUCHARIST: 1994

Some forty years later, on the day after the parish celebration of First Eucharist in 1994, Jean Carmody looks back on her experience. Jean is one of five catechists who worked with this year's group of twenty-five children and their parents. It was a good year, Jean thinks to herself. Most of the families were engaged and interested in the various events that she and the rest of the team offered.

The first meeting in October went well. It was there that the format and schedules for the year were set out and, most importantly, the parents were assured that they *can* teach their children about the faith. As a matter of fact, Jean remembers telling them that parents are always teaching their children about the faith whether they realize it or not! The adults who stayed to talk after the meeting continued their earlier conversation about how the Church's understanding of the sacraments developed in the years following Vatican II and how families and friends can play such important roles in continuing the initiation process with the children.

By mid-November Jean or one of the other catechists had visited the homes of all twenty-five children, giving each family a book of activities for parents and child to work on together. After skimming through the text, most parents seemed relieved that much of what they were asked to do was what they did anyway: tell stories about their own childhood and about the family, talk about their faith and its importance in their lives, and answer their son or daughter's questions about things that happened at Sunday liturgy. Jean recognizes that the need to talk with their son or daughter about Sunday liturgy was part of what got some of the parents coming to liturgy again. And having those special monthly liturgies that focused on a particular theme and emphasized one part of the liturgical celebration also helped. While she may not see some of the families very often after the First Eucharist celebration, Jean knows from past experience that the year's process is often a positive turning point for a number of families, affecting the degree of their participation in parish worship and activities.

This year they added the prayer cards — those really had worked well. The name of each child was printed on a small card, and a few short sentences proclaimed that he or she was preparing for further initiation into the community through Eucharist. Copies of the cards were left in the church entries, and people were invited to take one and to remember that child in prayer in a special way during the months of preparation. Many parishioners had commented on how nice it was to feel involved in the process even though they, themselves, didn't have a child preparing for First Eucharist. And people who were homebound genuinely appreciated the chance to feel connected to specific families in the community as they exercised their primary service to the parish through prayer! Joan Ryan had the right idea, Jean realizes. Joan made copies of her son's card and sent it to all the relatives — grandparents, aunts, and uncles — who are now living in various parts of the country. Many of them were able to gather for yesterday's celebration.

Undoubtedly, the most popular and effective part of this year's preparation program was the Saturday retreat for parents and children. Jean still could not decide which was the most favored of the activities: the bread-baking, the tour of the sacristy with all of the liturgical items set out and explained, or the quiet time each of the families had to talk about their own family traditions. At the conclusion of the day, each family filled in a small poster through which the parent and child agreed to some type of action or service that they could perform together for someone else. Sometimes the activity was fairly simple: visiting a relative in the hospital or helping a neighbor with yard work. Other times the family agreed to become involved in the wider community by working with the food shelf or getting involved in making meals for the homeless. And Jean is convinced that a number of the families really understood the connection between Eucharist and the call to work for justice.

Yes, Jean thinks, there are so many people and events in our lives that make the process of handing on our beliefs and traditions to the next generation so exciting!

In their reflections, both Sister Joseph Marie and Jean Carmody seem to be emphasizing the positive and effective elements of their tasks. And that is as it should be, as we are a people of hope! But a closer examination of their musings makes clear that they share more in common than their optimism. Clearly, each describes differently her central tasks, and the specific activities in which they engage are dissimilar. While Sister Joseph Marie speaks of religious instruction and teaching the children their catechism, Jean talks of faith formation and helping parents to tell the stories of our tradition. Although those differences are genuine, the similarity of what happens in the particular lives of these children and their families is striking.

It is possible to look at the two situations in this way: what Jean and the rest of her team worked to establish and support in 1994, Sister Joseph Marie could, in large measure, presume in 1954. Sister could presume that the majority of the children in her First Communion class of 1954 were members of churchgoing families. She could build on the fact that many of the parents were connected with the community through membership in church organizations or through joining with other parishioners for prayer. She could rely on extended family and neighbors to support the children and their parents in the preparation process. It is with these pieces in place that Sister Joseph Marie could be attentive to the children's instruction and explanation of the catechism, confident that most of the children experienced their faith at home with their families.

The situation for Jean and her team in 1994 is different. Jean and her contemporaries experience their roles and tasks differently from the way in which Sister Joseph Marie experienced hers in 1954. And that difference can be traced back to a number of changes, two of which are central to this discussion: first there have been significant changes in society and social structures; second, there have been shifts in the way the Church thinks about the process of forming ourselves in the faith. We can examine each in turn.

SOCIOLOGICAL CHANGES

To say that times have changed is in no way an adequate expression of the significant transformation that has taken place in all aspects of society and culture in the past forty years. The experiences of being a United States citizen, a Roman Catholic believer, and an inhabitant of Earth shifted radically in the years between 1954 and 1994. There is no need to enumerate and expand upon these profound social changes here. For this discussion, it is important to set out the social realities that account in part for the differences in self-understanding and approach that marked First Eucharist preparation for Sister Joseph Marie and for Jean.

John Westerhoff, in his book *Will Our Children Have Faith?*, explores these social changes by speaking of a "broken ecology." Westerhoff points out that in the past the interrelationship of extended family, homogeneous neighborhoods, church and school served to support and reinforce weekly catechetical instruction. It was presumed that the instruction dimension of catechesis was situated within the context of a believing community and implicitly strengthened and promoted by elements within family and social life.[1] This was the world within which Sister Joseph Marie prepared children for First Eucharist.

Even as we acknowledge the fundamental validity of this description, it is important that we not look back at the past too naively. Sister Joseph Marie's perception of the families of her second-grade students was probably not fully accurate. Certainly, few of her students' parents were divorced and fewer still were remarried. The number of students who came from single-parent families would have been small; and the number of mothers working outside the home would have been far less than the number in the families Jean worked with forty years later. Nonetheless, dysfunctional families existed in 1954 as well as in 1994. Our lack of awareness of detrimental family dynamics did not mean the problems did not exist; this lack of awareness often simply made it harder to discuss the difficulties and find support. In addition, the very dynamics that served to reinforce catechetical instruction — interrelationship of extended family, homogeneous neighborhoods, close connection between church and school — could also have a dark side. They also contributed to a milieu that could prevent people from genuinely examining the tradition into which they were socialized by creating a context in which it was virtually impossible to step back from one's faith in order to own it at a deeper level. And, in the past, these same realities have provided the setting for deep-seated prejudice against those who, because of their ethnic or racial background or their religious convictions, are outside the group.

Regardless of the strengths and flaws of this prior configuration of family, neighborhood, church and school, a range of social and cultural realities led to the disintegration of these elements. One can no longer presume that family, neighborhood, school and church all share a similar set of values; the sociological and religious "ecology" that was a part of the 1954 world is broken.

We might once have pictured a series of concentric circles with the family in the center surrounded and supported by neighborhood, school and church. But in the wake of this significant cultural shift, the picture has changed. We might better picture a series of independent circles that at times overlap but often share little in common. For catechesis, this means that one can no longer count on having weekly instruction supported by a foundation of extended family, neighborhoods, and schools with shared values and, often, common belief systems. Without a change in how we understand and give expression to catechesis, the burden of faith formation that had been upheld by these interrelated social structures all too often falls on a single dimension: weekly classroom experience.

It is clear from the earlier description of formation for the celebration of First Eucharist, that Jean's model differs significantly from that followed by Sister Joseph Marie. In 1994, Jean and her team of catechists see the importance of intentionally providing the opportunity for families to create in concert with others the support structures that Sister Joseph Marie simply presumed. In many ways Jean and her team are responding to the sociological change we just described. But for the basis of this change in approach, they can look not only to the sociological realities but to the dynamics that contributed to significant shifts in the Church's self-understanding. This shift is reflected in the documents of Vatican II and played out in a renewed understanding of catechesis.

CATECHETICAL RE-FOCUS

An understanding of the various movements present in the Church in the years leading up to the Second Vatican Council makes clear that the role of the council was not to introduce new ideas and insights but to recognize and affirm the expressions of the Spirit's presence in the life of the Church. The results of the council are expressed in the visible changes in Church practice — those connected with the renewal of liturgy are the most obvious. The impact of the council is also expressed in the more subtle shifts in theological understandings — the fundamental concept of revelation and the understanding of the nature of the Church are probably the most far-reaching of these.

But the antecedents and foundations of these changes and shifts can be found in the diverse expressions of the local church during the first half of this century. Long before the council and the renewal of the liturgy that followed from it, articles appeared in *Orate Fratres* (later *Worship*) concerning the use of the vernacular in the liturgy, and experimentation with the vernacular was taking place in some countries in Europe, Asia, and Latin America.[2] And long before the "Dogmatic Constitution on the Church" spoke of the fundamental image of the Church as the people of God, theologians like Yves Congar and Henri de Lubac were exploring the implications of such an image.[3] Bringing together the insights and needs of the Church as it was alive throughout the world served as an energy source for Vatican II. The council's greatness rests in its ability to recognize and affirm the presence of the Spirit in the life of the local church.

So, as we look to Vatican II as the ground and source of the refocusing of catechetics over the past forty years, it is important that we look back beyond the council to name more clearly the antecedents to this renewal in the first part of this century. What events, insights, and experiences serve as foundation for the refocusing of the task of catechesis?[4]

ATTENTION TO THE MESSAGE

A look back gives clarity to the evolution of our understanding of catechesis and brings into focus one of the key events of that evolution, the publication in 1936 of Josef Jungmann's *The Good News and Our Proclamation of the Faith*.[5] Although disapproval of its content by

Church authorities led to its withdrawal from circulation, this text along with other writings by Jungmann provided the foundation for a new understanding of the task of catechesis and the introduction of what came to be known as the kerygmatic movement.

In the years prior to the publication of Jungmann's book, the locus of interest in catechetical renewal was on the question of *method*. "How can we more effectively teach children the content of the catechism?" was the question asked by religion teachers at the turn of the century. Their question led to a reevaluation of the way in which children were taught and the introduction of a method that attempted to engage more effectively the learner's imagination and memory. By introducing the content of the lesson with a story or image the learners might remember, by focusing on one or two central ideas from the text's material, and by concluding with an attempt to make application of the content to the learners' lives, this method (referred to as the "Munich Method") attempted to facilitate learners' ability to understand and retain the catechism's content.[6]

Jungmann, however, argued that the main problem in catechesis was not the method that was being used but the *content* that was being presented. His concern and the concern reflected in the kerygmatic movement was that the *kerygma* or the core of the Christian message — the good news of the mystery of Christ — be at the heart of the catechetical endeavor. The compilation of propositions as presented in the catechisms of the day did little, Jungmann said, to incite learners to respond in faith to Christ. Looking back to the teaching of Christ and to the Emmaus story as the prime example of the potential impact of effective proclamation of the good news, Jungmann proposed this:

> There would seem to be a *law* here that has not been sufficiently appreciated at all times in our religious teaching: that it is not enough to show the necessity and reasonableness of the faith, nor enough to expound every point of doctrine and every commandment down to the very last division; but that it is singularly important to achieve first of all *a vital understanding* of the Christian message, bring together "the many" into a consistent, unified whole, that then *there may be joyous interest and enthusiastic response* in living faith.[7]

By attending to the "unity that lies behind 'the many,' the all-embracing salvific plan of God,"[8] catechesis is able to elicit from the learners a response of faith.

Jungmann's insight does not end in his proposal for a new way to perceive and present the Christian message. Jungmann made clear that the core of the Christian message cannot be presented solely through instruction. While instruction is important, it cannot stand alone. For Jungmann, the Scriptures as the story of God's saving action and the liturgy as the celebration of the paschal mystery are key elements to the proclamation of the Christian kerygma.[9] For Jungmann, the confluence of the biblical and liturgical renewals that were coming to the fore in the 1930s and '40s, complemented and energized the renewal of catechesis. Jungmann saw these renewals as fundamentally connected and as the foundation of a more general and wide-reaching pastoral renewal.

We cannot leave the discussion of the kerygmatic movement without making mention of Johannes Hofinger, the person most influential in disseminating Jungmann's essential insights. He shared with Jungmann a concern that a renewed focus be given to the message of catechesis and the doctrine that shaped the catechetical endeavor. For Hofinger, doctrine never stood alone but was to be integrated with liturgical and biblical catechesis. Reflective of a variety of other catechetical conversations taking place during the 1960s, Hofinger and those who picked up from him the insights of the kerygmatic movement recognized that catechesis requires a balance among the fourfold presentation of the faith — bible, liturgy, doctrine, and Christian witness.[10]

ATTENTION TO THE CONTEXT OF CATECHESIS

Hofinger's experience as a member of a seminary faculty in China during the late 1930s and early '40s set the foundation for his participation in what can be seen as a second reorientation in catechesis: not only are we to be concerned about the message, but attention must also be give to the *learner and the milieu* within which the learner experiences the good news. After the closing of the seminary in China, Hofinger participated with others in the founding of the East Asian Pastoral Institute. One of the Institute's most significant contributions to catechetics on an international level was the introduction of the international study weeks on missionary liturgy and catechetics held in various locations throughout the world from 1956 to 1968. It is at these international study weeks that the significance of the cultural context to the effectiveness of catechesis was brought into sharp focus in ways that challenged even Hofinger to expand his understanding of the tasks of the catechist in various cultural settings.

One of the conclusions of the International Study Week at Eichstatt in 1960 sets out the theme that is greatly expanded upon at other study weeks: "Catechesis adapts itself to the life and thought of the peoples, shows due appreciation of their laudable views and customs, and integrates them harmoniously into the Christian way of life."[11] Some eight years later — significant years for the Church with Vatican II and the promulgation of the council's documents — the International Study Week at Medellin makes clear the importance of renewed attention to the learner's milieu.

> Contemporary catechesis, in agreement with a more adequate theology of revelation, recognizes in historical situations and in authentic human aspirations the first sign to which we must be attentive in order to discover the plan of God for the men and women of today. Such situations, therefore, are an indispensable part of the content of catechesis.[12]

The cultural context and historical situation of the learner is not simply where catechesis takes place; it is at the heart of the content of catechesis.

In this brief review of the evolution of catechesis during this century, we have traced the shift in emphasis from a concern for the method of religious instruction to a reexamination of the message or content of catechesis, to a recognition of the context or milieu within which catechesis takes place.[13] Each phase has drawn from and built upon the strengths and insights of the previous periods. And in some ways, each phase is anticipated and present in nascent form in the phase prior to it.

THE COMMUNITY AS AGENT OF CATECHESIS

So where does that leave us as we speak about catechesis today? What are the focus and contributions of contemporary conversations about catechesis? I propose that we are moving into a new phase involving a shift of focus from the previous phase's concern for the question "Who is the learner and how is the learner's milieu at the heart of catechesis?" to "Who is the agent of catechesis; who has the responsibility for fostering faith?'' This phase builds upon the recognition that catechesis takes place not only — and not even primarily — within an instructional setting.

It is not primarily instruction, but the very life of the faith community that shapes and forms our faith, that clarifies and defines our beliefs. It is the very life of the faith community that gives expression to the story of who we are as a people. It is within the Christian community that we recognize that this is not just a story, just the history of a people. We recognize that this story forms the identity of a specific community, is celebrated in particular forms of prayer and worship, and is given expression in a certain way of life.

Who, then, is the agent of catechesis? It is the very life of the community as it gathers to remember and retell the Christian story, as it celebrates the Christian story within the liturgy, and as it lives out the story in a life marked by gospel values.

This emphasis on the community as agent of catechesis does not discount the role of instruction. We continue to build on the insights of the previous phases. But it does put instruction into a much larger context. To say that the community is the agent of catechesis involves a recognition that central to the catechetical enterprise are the various means by which the community gives expression to itself. Formation in faith involves participation with the community as it is shaped by the gospel story, as it proclaims and teaches the story, as it gives expression to that through liturgy, as it expands the gospel story beyond itself in efforts to work for justice.[14]

These expressions of Church life — living in community, proclaiming and teaching, praying and worshiping, and engaging in service — are the fundamental expression of the faith into which we are formed and the means by which formation takes place. The very action of participating in the life of the community deepens the individual's incorporation into the community and enhances his or her appropriation of the community's values and world-view. By entering into experiences of prayer and worship, the members of the community are shaped into people of prayer. With this understanding of the dynamics of catechesis, it becomes clear that the primary agent of catechesis is the very life of the community. The entire community as it gathers, preaches, teaches, prays, and serves is faith formative.

Naming the community as the agent of catechesis invites us to make significant shifts in perspective. No longer is catechesis seen as simply instruction about the ways in which the community gave life to the gospel vision in the past and into the present; the various ways in which the community expresses the gospel message is more than simply the content of that instruction. Catechesis involves engaging with the ways in which faith comes to expression within our community — communal living, proclamation, teaching, liturgy, and service, — and seeing those as both the context and expression of catechesis, as well as its content.

A second shift involves the recognition of the fundamental interconnection of these elements. To say that the community is the agent of catechesis entails seeing the unity of these often separate elements of community, story, liturgy, and service. No longer can these elements be seen as discreet topics that can or must be taught. They are an integrated whole, a part of the life of the community that shapes us into people with living, conscious, and active faith.

In addition, a third shift is involved. The question is changed from "How we are to cover all of these topics in our time of instruction?" to "How are we to live within these dimensions of Christian life and learn to reflect on that living?" Once we recognize the community as the agent of catechesis, it becomes clear that the content of catechesis is not something we give or present to the learners, but rather a reality that we attempt to live out and incarnate within the life of the community.

CATECHESIS AND THE CATECHISM

We entered into this exercise of identifying the dynamics of catechesis with the intention of more clearly naming the place of a catechism within this endeavor. This excursion into the history of catechesis has given us a way of understanding the differences in approach to formation for the celebration of Eucharist described in the opening pages. Jean and her team of catechists in 1994 are providing the learners — adults and children — with the opportunity to enter more intentionally into the basic expressions of the faith community. By participating in community, teaching, liturgy, and service, those preparing for the Eucharistic celebration are being formed into a eucharistic people.

And what does this say about the place of a catechism in contemporary catechesis? It clearly serves a more complex role than the role it was given in the past. Given our discussion of the nature of the catechetical endeavor, the Catechism does not serve simply as the source of the content of catechesis. We can think of the text as providing direction or focus as we enter into the dynamics of community life. As we engage in faith formation by entering into the various expressions of Church life, the *Catechism* serves to root us within a broader tradition. For example, faith formation takes place in the context of the community gathered for prayer, in the context of liturgy. But the formative role of the liturgy has a depth beyond a particular faith community gathered on a particular Sunday morning. The foundation for the liturgy's formative role is built on the understandings, insights, and experiences of liturgy that have shaped our tradition. These insights and experiences have been refocused for us in the documents of Vatican II, particularly in the *Constitution on the Sacred Liturgy*. The *Catechism* serves as a significant point of reference as we attempt to more clearly name the foundational insights that shape our understanding and experience of liturgy today.

The *Catechism* can serve a similar role as we look to the formative effect of service. Participation in action for justice is itself formative: we are shaped into a people of justice. But the understanding of the significance of that is rooted in a tradition of teaching on social justice. This teaching has become explicit over the past century, beginning with *Rerum Novarum* and continuing through *Centesimus Annus*. An examination of the evolution of the Church's social teaching provides the foundation for our more intentional entrance into the formative work of justice. The *Catechism* provides an explication of that tradition.

The *Catechism*, then, is neither the sum of what catechesis is about nor is it merely the sourcebook for the content of the instructional dimension of catechesis. As a text with the aim of "presenting an organic synthesis of the essential and fundamental contents of Catholic doctrine" (CCC 11), it serves as a key resource in illumining the ways in which the Church gives shape to the good news today. Those "essential and fundamental contents" function to define the parameters within which we come to understand the various dimensions of the Christian life — who we are as a community, what is the story we share, how do we express that story in prayer, how is that story expanded in service to others. As an "organic synthesis," it provides a framework for recognizing the fundamental unity among the various dynamics within the faith community as each gives expression to the dimensions of the Christian story lived out today.

Notes for Chapter 1

1. Westerhoff, John, *Will Our Children Have Faith?* (Minneapolis, Minn.: Seabury, 1976) 13–15.

2. The papers presented at the International Study Week on Mission and Liturgy held in Nijmegen, Holland, September 1959, contain multiple references to the need for the vernacular in the liturgy. The appendix to the published papers is entitled "Examples of Privileges Regarding the Use of the Vernacular Granted by Rome in Recent Years." Johannes Hofinger, ed., *Liturgy and the Missions: The Nijmegen Papers* (Collegeville, Minn.: The Liturgical Press, 1960) 293–295.

3. In the book *Lay People in the Church*, trans. D. Attwater (Westminster, Md.: Newman Press, 1957), which first appeared in 1953, Yves Congar discussed the role of the laity within his understanding of the Church as the people of God. His understanding of this concept is developed in his book *Mystery of the Temple*, trans. R.F. Trevett (Westminster, Md.: Newman Press, 1962). One can find antecedents to the concepts Congar explores in the writings of Henri de Lubac. See particularly, chapter II, "The Church," in *Catholicism: A Study of Dogma in Relation to the Corporate Destiny of Mankind* (London: Burns, Oates and Washbourne, 1950).

4. Several articles collected by Michael Warren in *Sourcebook for Modern Catechesis* (Winona, Minn.: St. Mary's Press, 1983) provide insight into this period of catechesis. Particularly helpful are the articles by Luis Erdozain ("The Evolution of Catechetics: A Survey of Six International Study Weeks on Catechetics") and by Berard Marthaler ("The Modern Catechetical Movement in Roman Catholicism: Issues and Personalities"). See also Kenneth Barker "Historical Background" in *Religious Education, Catechesis and Freedom* (Birmingham, Ala.: Religious Education Press, 1981), particularly pp. 34–62.

5. Because of the controversy surrounding Jungmann's book, it was not translated into English until 1962, under the title *The Good News Yesterday and Today* (New York: Sadlier, 1962). Included with the translation of Jungmann's text are essays that appraise Jungmann's contribution to the catechetical movement.

6. Jungmann discusses the "Munich Method" and the difficulties of the approach in the chapter "The History of Catechesis" in *Handing on the Faith: A Manual of Catechetics* (New York: Herder and Herder, 1959).

7. *Good News Yesterday and Today*, 6

8. Ibid., 8.

9. The important role of liturgy is clearly set out in "Divine Worship," chapter in *The Good News Yesterday and Today*. For a discussion of the role of Scripture, see Jungmann, *Announcing the Word of God*, trans. Ronald Walls (London: Burns and Oates, 1967) 8–15, and Jungmann, "Christ's Place in Catechesis and Preaching," *Lumen Vitae* 7 (1952) 533–42.

10. The integration of these four "signs" of catechesis was seen as essential to modern catechesis at the International Study Weeks at Eichstatt (1960) and Bangkok (1962). See Alfonso Nebreda's summary of the insights of the East Asian Study Week on Mission Catechesis in Bangkok in 1962 in Michael Warren, *Sourcebook for Modern Catechetics*, 40–53. As Kenneth Barker points out in his discussion of the contribution of Jungmann and Hofinger to contemporary catechesis, "these four 'signs' or 'languages' of catechesis have their root in Jungmann's work. . . ." Kenneth Barker, *Religious Education, Catechesis and Freedom*, 51.

11. "Basic Principles of Modern Catechetics: A Summary Report from Eichstatt," in Warren, *Sourcebook*, 38. Reprinted from Appendix III of *Teaching All Nations: A Symposium on Modern Catechetics*, Johannes Hofinger and Clifford Howell, eds. (New York: Herder and Herder, 1961) 394–400.

12. "General Conclusions of the Medellin International Study Week: 1968," in Warren, *Sourcebook*, 68. Reprinted from *The Medellin Papers*, Johannes Hofinger and Terence J. Sheridan, eds. (East Asian Pastoral Institute, 1969) 213–219.

13. In an article written shortly before his death, Johannes Hofinger presents his summary of the evolution of catechesis along similar lines. At the conclusion of the article, Hofinger proposes a fourth phase of catechesis. Hofinger describes this phase as the "spiritual" phase that places an emphasis on the spiritual foundation of the catechist him/herself. "Looking Backward and Forward: Journey of Catechesis," *The Living Light* 20 (June 1984) 349–358.

14. A number of catechetical theorists have explored this broader vision of the catechetical endeavor. One of the more sustained and clearest expressions of this is given by Maria Harris in her book *Fashion Me a People: Curriculum in the Church* (Louisville: Westminster/John Knox Press, 1989). In the final section of *Sharing Faith: A Comprehensive Approach to Religious Education and Pastoral Ministry* (San Francisco: Harper Collins, 1991) Thomas Groome uses these four elements — *kerygma, koinōnia, leitourgia,* and *diakōnia* — to speak of the fundamental elements of Christian ministry. In *Weaving the New Creation* (San Francisco: Harper, 1991), James Fowler uses these categories (plus *paideia*) to examine the key dimensions of a Christian community's life and mission. In each case, the writers see these as essential elements of the dynamics of the Christian community.

II. The Context of History

CHAPTER 2

The Catechism: "Inspired by the Great Tradition of Catechisms"

> The plan of this catechism is inspired by the great tradition of catechisms that build on four pillars: the baptismal profession of faith (the Creed), the sacraments of faith, the life of faith (the commandments), and the prayer of the believer (the Lord's Prayer) — CCC 13.

Advent 1985 brought with it the conclusion of the Extraordinary Synod that had been meeting in Rome. While there had been some discussion in the popular press and in Catholic periodicals concerning the synod's deliberation, the topic that received a good deal of attention was the discussion of a catechism. Reactions to the proposal for a universal catechism varied widely in the Church in the United States and elsewhere. Whether their response to the proposal was one of welcome or dread, whether they thought that the future catechism should be embraced or ignored, people seemed quite clear about what they thought they were reacting to — a catechism. Everyone knows what a catechism is.

In the synod's Final Report, as well as in the closing address given by Pope John Paul II, reference is made to the preparation of "a compendium or catechism of all Catholic doctrine. . . ."[1] The popular press, as well as more scholarly writings, picked up on the term "catechism" rather than "compendium," and that has become the dominant term. At some level, that makes sense: the term "catechism" has been in use throughout Church history; we have a sense of what it refers to.

For many the idea of catechism brings to mind a book designed for learners, usually children, presented in a question and answer format. This experience or understanding of catechism shaped our expectations of the catechism proposed by the 1985 synod.

This picture of what a catechism is, however, reflects just one aspect of the catechism genre. The Christian Church has from the beginning attempted to set out a "catechism or compendium of all Catholic doctrine." And these texts have taken many forms. To illuminate more clearly the appropriate role of the *Catechism of the Catholic Church* as it was proposed by the synod, and to name the significant issues and questions the publication of a catechism raises, we here examine the history of the evolution of the catechism genre.

Examining the times in history when the call for a catechism came to the fore, exploring the evolution of the format of the text, and discussing the relationship between the catechism and catechesis as it came to expression at various times in the Church's history: all of these will provide insights helpful to our reading of this particular catechism, the *Catechism of the Catholic Church.*

EARLY CATECHISMS

As we begin this foray into history, it is important that we name the criteria for including some texts and excluding others. What is the basis for labeling a particular work a catechism? While the history of Christianity includes many attempts to express the central teachings of the tradition, for our discussion we can speak here of catechism as a text written with some specific intention of presenting a systematic exposition of core doctrine that aims to facilitate or enhance catechesis.

Many of the early works which are catechetical in nature and which attempt to set out the central concepts of Catholic belief were not, in fact, originally designed for the written format. Here we can think of the pre-baptismal and mystagogical lectures of Cyril of Jerusalem, for example, or the homilies of John Chrysostom. These collections of lectures and homilies highlight the centrality of the oral presentation of the Christian message and make clear that the primary recipient of catechesis is the adult community.

On the other hand, some of the written texts were not intended as inclusive presentations of Catholic teaching. The writings of Augustine against Pelagianism, those of Ambrose on the sacraments, and Origen's commentary on the Gospel of John: each of these is an example of a written work designed to challenge a particular heresy or affirm a specific practice. As will be evident when we examine catechisms more closely, the genre is, at some level, always apologetic in nature.

Thus, while not catechisms per se, these writings provide insight into the questions of the day and a context for understanding more general works such as a catechism. Insight into the divisive issues contemporary with a particular catechism is an important element in interpreting the text.

As we look to the period from the early Church up to the beginning of the Middle Ages, two texts that correspond to our description of a catechism stand out: Gregory of Nyssa's *Catechetical Instruction*, or *Great Catechism*, written sometime before 385 and Augustine's *Enchiridion*, completed about 421.[2] Both of these texts are explicitly catechetical in nature and represent some attempt to set out the principles of Catholic teaching; they serve as good examples of the catechism-type texts of the era.[3]

The opening lines of Gregory of Nyssa's *Catechetical Instruction* make clear the focus of this catechism:

> The presiding ministers of the "mystery of godliness" have need of a system in their instruction, in order that the Church may be replenished by the accession of such as should be saved, through the teaching of the word of Faith being brought home to the hearing of unbelievers.[4]

The leaders, here particularly bishops, have the responsibility to teach the word of faith to unbelievers. Essential to the task is a "system in their instruction," a synthesis of the central teachings of the tradition, and a means of presentation that leads to faith. The remainder of the prologue reminds the catechist that the teaching of the faith must be adapted to the hearer. Gregory writes:

> Not that the same method of instruction will be suitable in the case of all who approach the word. The catechism must be adapted to the diversities of their religious worship; with an eye, indeed, to the one aim and end of the system, but not using the same method of preparation in each individual case.[5]

He then enumerates various perspectives and heresies that shape the hearer's ability to attend to the teachings and proposes lines of questioning and reasoning that might appeal to each.

The main section of the text can be divided into three sections. The first sets out the central teaching on the Trinity, which is rooted in the reality of creation and finds foundation in analogy to human nature. The second section examines the nature of the incarnation and its "reasonableness" to both Judaism and Hellenism. The final section argues for the importance of the sacraments of baptism and the Eucharist and their connection with the Trinity. The final chapter of *Catechetical Instruction* points out to the reader that "the instruction of this Catechism does not seem to me to be yet complete" without some discussion of the need for conversion expressed in a change of life.

Like Gregory of Nyssa's text, Augustine's *Enchiridion* is designed to present a summation of central elements of the Christian tradition. Augustine's text is a response to a request from a friend, Laurentius, who asks for a handbook responding to such questions as:

> What is most to be sought after? In view of various heresies, what is chiefly to be avoided? To what extent does matter known through faith alone not fall under the scope of reason? What is the beginning and what the end of human endeavor? What is the sum total of all teaching? What is the sure and true foundation of Catholic faith?[6]

In responding to these questions, Augustine writes: "All these things that you ask about you will undoubtedly know if you understand well what man should believe and hope for and love."[7] He then sets out to explore these elements by examining the baptismal Creed, the Lord's Prayer, and the Great Commandment of Love.

The Creed serves as the organizing principle for the majority of the text; Augustine examines the basic theme of each of the articles, including digressions as he deems necessary. Toward the end of the text is a brief examination of the Lord's Prayer as the summary of that for which the Christian is to hope. A comparison of the version in the Gospels of Matthew and Luke gives Augustine the means for highlighting the prayer's central meaning. The final two chapters of the *Enchiridion* examine the call to charity that is embodied in love of God and love of neighbor.

While these are just two of a number of texts one might consider "catechisms" from this early period, this brief account of these two texts provides us with some insights into this genre as it was envisioned in its earliest form. First, both of these texts make clear that, whatever their lasting value, catechisms are written in response to a particular time and place. Neither Gregory nor Augustine is attempting to present an ahistorical expression of Christian doctrine. Both writers acknowledge and address the various issues and heresies of their day. Gregory's "Prologue" makes clear his conscious attention to the various distortions of the faith that were present at the time. Augustine's extensive discussions of evil, sin, and the free gift of grace echo his earlier battles with heresies such as those expressed in Manichaeism and Pelagianism. It is essential that catechisms be read within their historical context.

Secondly, both writers presume the essential role of the catechist in teaching the faith. Augustine concludes his introductory comments concerning the content of the *Enchiridion* by making clear that the handbook itself is not enough.

> And to impart such instruction, it will not suffice to place a small manual in one's hand; rather it will be necessary to enkindle a great zeal in one's heart.[8]

It is the catechist's task not only to present the central elements of Christian teaching but to do so in such a way as to evoke a response of faith. The catechism is a tool in that broader process.

Finally, the schemes of both texts conclude with a call to the moral life. Augustine's discussion of charity and Gregory's injunction to express regeneration through a change in one's life point to the essential purpose of instruction: a life lived in response to God's grace. Knowledge and affirmation of the teaching is seen as genuine when reflected in a faith-filled life.

CATECHISMS OF THE MIDDLE AGES

An examination of written works that appear during the Middle Ages makes clear the influence of Augustine's writings. The three-part division of his handbook, the use he makes of Scripture, and the connection he makes between the Ten Commandments, or the Decalogue, and the core commandment of love of God and love of neighbor: these all are evident to some extent in catechisms of the early Middle Ages. The period we are exploring here begins with the rule of Charlemagne in the ninth century and continues to the time of the Reformation in the sixteenth century. Three aspects are important to our discussion here: concern about clergy education, the development of works for common people, and focus on children.

Catechisms for the Clergy

Concern about the education level of clergy and preparation of the clergy for preaching has often served as an impetus for the preparation of catechisms. With the tenth-century mandate that clergy have sole responsibility for preaching, the need for some type of handbook or catechism was evident. Texts designed for clergy and other educated adults were written throughout the Middle Ages.

For the English-speaking clergy, the foundational source for this type of work can be found in the writing of John Pecham, archbishop of Canterbury. Following the directive of the Lambeth Council of 1281, Pecham prepared "On the Instruction of Simple Folk," in which he sets out the importance of teaching the fundamentals of the faith. The content that Pecham proposes is similar to that of Thomas Aquinas, who presented a series of homilies around several topics: the commandment of love, the Ten Commandments, the Apostles' Creed, and the Lord's Prayer. Later authors added to Pecham's work such topics as the seven virtues and deadly sins, the seven acts of mercy, and the sacraments.[9]

A dynamic that played a significant role in the creation of these handbooks or catechisms, and on the evolution of catechesis, was the connection drawn between catechesis and the sacrament of penance and reconciliation. The Fourth Lateran Council (1215) mandated annual confession to one's pastor; it also emphasized the importance of instruction and the central responsibility that clergy had in this task. Pastorally, these two directives became linked: priests were instructed to quiz people on their knowledge of the tradition when they came for their annual confession. Most often, persons were required to recite the Lord's Prayer, the Creed, and the Ten Commandments prior to confession. As this practice evolved, instruction in the faith became increasingly linked with confession, and issues of morality began to receive considerable emphasis. Examinations of conscience were often integrated into these catechetical guides for the clergy.

Catechisms for the People

While texts designed to educate the clergy and to guide preaching were popular throughout this period, there was also a collection of texts prepared for the use of those less educated. These catechisms are particularly significant because they advance the question-and-answer format and provide an increasingly simplified rendition of the Christian message.

The *Elucidarium* (subtitled "Summary of All Christian Theology") is one of the more influential texts that incorporate the question-answer format.[10] Written in the twelfth century, it gives firm evidence of the move away from the emphasis in early Church catechesis on initiation toward a more dogmatic approach to communicating the tradition. The text, designed for adults, is divided into three books: the nature of God and the role of the sacraments, sin and concupiscence, and the "last things," with particular attention to the fate of the damned and the blessed. While impressive in its scope and clarity, the *Elucidarium* must be viewed with some misgivings: it serves as a precursor to later texts which tended to present simplified and at times simplistic answers or statements and to present the Christian mystery as distinct propositions suitable for memorization.

Symptomatic of this move toward simplification and memorization was the rise of mnemonics designed to aid the illiterate in learning core teachings. Probably one of the best and most influential examples is Hugh of St. Victor's small work, *De quinque septenis seu septenariis*, which is dated in the early twelfth century. Setting out sacred truths under the heading of "five sevens," Hugh lists the capital sins, the petitions of the Lord's Prayer, the gifts of the Holy Spirit, the virtues, and the Beatitudes. For those already familiar with these foundational elements, Hugh's work gives insight into their fundamental relationships; for example, he draws parallels between the vices and the petitions of the Lord's Prayer. However, for those less knowledgeable about the tradition, this work tends to be uninspiring and overly simplistic.

The texts mentioned here, and others like them, reflect attempts to provide catechesis to an uneducated and generally illiterate society. As such, they are a positive sign of the Church's attentiveness to the needs of the faithful. Unfortunately, in later years, when taken out of the context of the medieval culture, these served to limit the learners' entry into the mystery of Christ and entangled them instead in lists and propositions unconnected with lived faith.[11]

Catechisms and Children

Throughout the first thousand years of the Church's existence, it was presumed that instruction in the faith had an adult focus. The shift toward including children in the process of catechesis came to the fore in the late Middle Ages. Among the most articulate proponent of catechesis for children is John Gerson, who lived in France in the late fourteenth and early fifteenth centuries. Even while chancellor of the University of Paris, Gerson engaged in catechesis. During the later years of his life in Lyons, he focused particularly on the importance of catechesis for children.

Reflective of his era, Gerson placed strong emphasis on preaching, teaching, and especially confession. Gerson's *Opus Tripertitum,* designed primarily for instructing children and uneducated adults, contains an introduction on creation, the Trinity, and God's saving grace, in addition to the three major sections that examine the commandments, confession, and how to die well. His "ABC for Simple Folk" includes the Our Father, the Hail Mary, the Creed, the Ten Commandments, and the seven virtues and vices.

One suggestion that Gerson made gives evidence of his concern for the less educated and for children: he recommended the use of charts or tables listing the central elements of doctrine or specifying various kinds of sins. These were to be hung in churches so that those preparing for confession might review them and thus be prepared for the priest's questions on basic prayers and Church teaching.

This brief review of catechisms or catechetical texts of the Middle Ages gives evidence of the efforts invested in addressing the instructional needs of the people of the period. The double focus on the education of the clergy and their readiness for preaching, on the one hand, and the needs of the less educated and children, on the other, gave rise to a range of very different books. But in each kind of book, there was a growing interest in lists and propositions. Along with this, the development of the question-and-answer genre led to oversimplification and a tendency to separate doctrine from daily Christian living.

As we move into the Reformation period and the subsequent proliferation of catechisms, these issues and concerns do not fade away. They move to center stage, as the members of each faction make attempts to clarify their position and to teach the truth to others.

THE REFORMATION PERIOD: EXPANSION OF THE CATECHISM GENRE

A number of different types of texts have been examined in this historical review of the evolution of the catechism. Each of them fulfills the basic description of a catechism set forth in the beginning of this chapter: a text written with some specific intention of presenting a systematic exposition of core doctrine that aims to facilitate or enhance catechesis. As we turn our attention to the period following the Reformation, two shifts are noteworthy: first, the term "catechism" comes to designate a particular type of text and, second, these texts take on specific roles in the wake of the Reformation.

It is impossible to catalogue and describe all the various catechisms that were composed for use by groups formed and transformed by the Reformation. We can, however, explore the format, structure, and importance of the catechisms of the era by looking closely at three of the more significant sets of catechisms: those of Martin Luther, those of Peter Canisius, and the catechism of the Council of Trent. These are significant because they were among the first written in light of the Reformation, and they served as models for later catechism into the nineteenth century.

Catechisms of Martin Luther

Once the Reformed Church had gained some stability, the task of defining the core beliefs and establishing a shared identity was addressed. As early as 1525 — just ten years after Luther posted his ninety-five theses on the Wittenberg door, thus setting the Reformation in motion — Luther asked some of his followers to compose a book of instruction for children. These early attempts met with no success; in 1529 Luther composed the "German Catechism" (or "Large Catechism") designed for adults responsible for instructing children and uneducated adults, and the "Small Catechism" suitable for children and beginners.[12]

Most of the catechisms or catechetical manuals prepared up to this point followed a somewhat predictable pattern: many of them following the schema set down by Augustine of Creed, Lord's Prayer, and Commandments. In contrast to this, Martin Luther's "Large Catechism" begins with the Ten Commandments and then proceeds to a discussion of the Creed and the Lord's Prayer. These three he describes as "the most necessary parts of Christian instruction."[13] These three main parts are followed by an explication of baptism and the sacrament of the altar. A section on preparation for confession was added in some later editions.

Luther's rationale for the arrangement is made clear in the text: The commandments set out God's expectations, what humans must do to follow the divine plan. Given the realities of human nature, no one is able to follow these directives and so all are condemned. It is in the Creed and the Lord's Prayer that humans find hope. Through the Creed and the Lord's Prayer the person learns what to believe and how to pray in order to be strengthened for the task of following the commandments. For Luther, the law (set out in the Ten Commandments) indicts; faith (expressed in the Creed and the Lord's Prayer) saves. For Luther, the very structure of the catechism highlights the fundamental presuppositions of Christian life.

Catechisms of Peter Canisius

Following a somewhat different schema are the catechisms written by the Jesuit Peter Canisius. Using the advice of Sirach — "If you desire wisdom, keep the commandments, and the Lord will bestow her upon you" (Sirach 1:23) — Canisius divided his major catechism into two sections headed "Wisdom" and "Justice." Under "Wisdom" he followed the plan that Augustine had used, exploring faith, hope, and charity through an explication of the Creed, the Lord's Prayer, and the Hail Mary, and the Decalogue and Precepts of the Church. The first section concludes with a chapter on sacraments, which are seen as the means for coming to wisdom and for "keeping" justice. The "Justice" section includes a discussion of the evils to be avoided (seven capital sins, sins against the Holy Spirit, for example) and good that must be attained (works of mercy, cardinal virtues, Beatitudes, etc.). Between 1555 and 1559 Canisius wrote three catechisms. Like Luther he wrote a large one for those versed in the Catholic tradition and able to follow simple theological discourse, as well as two smaller ones for use by children and those less educated.[14]

It is helpful to our discussion of the nature of catechisms to delineate the differences between the "large" and "small" catechisms. They differ significantly in audience, format, and intent. The "large" catechisms have as their audience the educated adult and often the adult who has responsibility for teaching others. Luther's "Large Catechism" is clearly addressed to preachers and parents. After listing the three necessary parts of Christian education — the Ten Commandments, the Creed, and the Lord's Prayer — Luther admonishes the reader:

> We should learn to repeat them word for word. Our children should be taught the habit of reciting them daily when they rise in the morning, when they go to meals, and when they go to bed at night; until they repeat them they should not be given anything to eat or drink. Every father has the same duty to his household; he should dismiss man-servants and maid-servants if they do not know these things and are unwilling to learn them.[15]

In the discussion of the various commandments or articles in the Creed, Luther proposes for the reader ways to respond to questions that the unlearned may ask. On the other hand, the audience for the "small" catechisms consists of children and the unlearned. The smallest catechism that Canisius wrote consisted of fifty-nine questions and answers and included prayer texts to be used at various times during the day. This small catechism first appeared as an appendix to a Latin grammar. A somewhat larger edition designed for children in lower and middle grades appeared in 1558.

The audience gives shape to the form. The "small" catechisms are in the format that many people connect with the catechism genre: questions and answers. The questions walk the reader through the basic topics of the Christian tradition, and the answers are given in short, concise phrases that are suitable for memorization. In many "small" catechisms, these short statements are followed by paragraphs that provide more detail. The "large" catechisms, on the other hand, seldom have questions and responses. They are more theological than catechetical in nature, though some "large" catechisms include sections with recommendations for presenting or preaching the material in the text. Designed for the more educated — at times specifically for the clergy — the "large" catechisms include lengthy discussions of doctrinal points.

The intention or aim of the two models of catechisms also differs somewhat. While the "small" catechism is clearly designed to present a summary of Christian belief, its intention is also to form the identity of the learner around Christian teaching. It is in the memorization of Commandments, Creed, and Lord's Prayer, as well as the responses to these central questions, that the child becomes inculcated with the Christian view of the world. Luther's "Small Catechism" and that of Canisius were often presented in the context of prayer books, thus heightening the formative role. The "large" catechism generally has the intention of presenting a synthesized rendition of key elements of the Christian tradition. Those catechisms prepared in the wake of the Reformation were often apologetic in nature, emphasizing and clarifying the positions that had been challenged by those opposed. In that sense, the "large" catechism becomes a point of orthodoxy, a touchstone to verify right belief.

Catechism of the Council of Trent

The prime example of a "large" catechism is the one written following the Council of Trent.[16] Often referred to as the "Roman Catechism" this text is clearly addressed to clergy, with the intention of providing guidance for their task of presenting the Catholic faith through preaching and instruction. The introduction makes clear that the writers' purpose is not to present all of Christian teaching but to treat such things

> . . . as might assist the pious zeal of pastors in discharging the duty of instruction, should they not be very familiar with the more abstruse questions of theology.[17]

The introduction then includes sections describing "the ends of religious instruction" (knowledge of Christ, observance of the commandments, and love of God), "the means required for religious instruction" (instruction accommodated to the capacity of the hearer, zeal, study of the word of God) and a description of the parts of the catechism.

Divided into four parts, the catechism consists of discussions of the Creed, the sacraments, the commandments, and the Lord's Prayer. A comparison of this schema to that of Augustine (Creed, Lord's Prayer, and Commandment of Love) gives indication of the relative importance that the Roman Catechism places on the sacraments. This sequence clearly situates the sacraments at the heart of Christian life and belief.

The concern for religious instruction and the pastoral presentation of the content of the catechism that is evident in the introduction continues throughout the text itself. The beginning of each of the articles of the Creed, for example, includes a paragraph discussing its significance. In the opening paragraph of Article VI: "He ascended into heaven, sits at the right hand of God, the Father Almighty'' is this directive:

> . . . he [the pastor] should take care that the people not only perceive it with faith and understanding, but that they also strive as far as possible, with the Lord's help, to reflect it in their lives and actions.[18]

In various places in the text there are also some recommendations for the most effective method for presenting a particular teaching. Directions are also given to the pastor concerning other Church writings, particularly the early Church Fathers, which provide further discussion of a specific teaching.

Clearly pastoral in its intent, structure, and content, the Roman Catechism reflected accurately the understanding and world view that shaped the Catholic response to the Reformation. Used as a resource for preaching and teaching, the Roman Catechism along with other reforms that stemmed from the Council of Trent, contributed significantly to the renewal of the Church in the years following the Reformation.

There are other catechisms that came to the fore in the second half of the sixteenth century. Among the better known are those of Robert Bellarmine published in 1597 and 1598. His "small" catechism follows the usual Augustinian schema of Creed, Lord's Prayer, Commandments, and the sacraments. The "large" catechism is a companion to the smaller, serving as a teacher's manual of sorts. Bellarmine's catechism attained great popularity in Italy and beyond and was seen as a possible model for catechisms composed into the twentieth century.

This overview of Reformation catechisms provides some insights into the nature of the catechism that can be of help to our conversation here. First, the distinction between a "large" and "small" catechism is important to keep in mind in interpreting the *Catechism of the Catholic Church*. Noting that it has been written in the tradition of the "large" catechism gives some direction as to how it is to be interpreted and used.

Secondly, while the topics explored in most of these catechisms were fairly similar, the sequence of their presentation differed at times. This leads us to ask questions concerning the schema and structure of the *Catechism*. What is the significance of the fact that the sequence of the

Catechism of the Catholic Church is the same as that of the Roman Catechism? In what ways do the schema and structure of the *Catechism* give us a key for interpreting the text?

Finally, history tells us that neither Luther's catechism nor the catechism of the Council of Trent brought about or stabilized any reform. These catechisms were but one part of broader cultural and ecclesial changes; the catechisms both contributed to and reflected these transformations but were not the only or even main source. As we look at the *Catechism of the Catholic Church* we need to ask about the other elements in the life of the Church that contribute to catechesis and to growth in faith. This catechism is part of a larger reality in which it must be situated and through which it must be interpreted.

But before we move to a closer examination of our contemporary catechism, let us complete our historical review with a discussion of catechisms from the Reformation to the present.

TOWARD THE MODERN CATECHISM

During the century following the Reformation, dozens of Roman Catholic catechisms were written and circulated. While they varied in title and author, for the most part they reflected one or another of the early catechisms — that of Canisius, perhaps, or of Bellarmine. As we scan these next few centuries, two developments are worth noting: first, the development of catechisms that reflected a sensitivity to the method of catechesis, and second, a growing concern about the multiplication of catechisms in this country and elsewhere.

A number of catechisms that were developed in the seventeenth century moved beyond those of the Reformation in an attempt to more adequately address methodological concerns. The most significant of these is undoubtedly that written by Claude Fleury in 1683. For Fleury, the issue was not simply the addition of more content or the inclusion of an introduction that reviewed basic catechetical principles and techniques. Fleury's *Catéchisme Historique* incorporates the ancient tradition of imparting the faith in the context of the story of God's action in human history.

Fleury's catechism actually is two catechisms in one. The "Small Catechism" consists of two parts. The first sets out Christian doctrine in the classic four sections that characterized other catechisms: Creed, Lord's Prayer, the Ten Commandments and Precepts of the Church, and the sacraments. The second part presents a summary of "salvation history," beginning with the Bible and continuing through the evolution of the Church up through the development of monasticism. The second catechism, the "Great Catechism," designed for the instruction of adults and those teaching younger learners, follows the same sequence, expounding further on the basic ideas presented in the "Small Catechism."

In his lengthy preface, Fleury sets out the rationale for his own catechism and, in doing so, criticizes the catechisms of his day in their use of theoretical categories and scholastic language. For Fleury, catechesis is rooted in the narrative that gives context and significance to the catechism's teaching. Not only is it important to know those events that have doctrinal significance: the story of creation, the story of Moses and the giving of the Ten Commandments, for example. It is also important to gain a knowledge of the flow of sacred history and the people and places that shape the story of salvation. In addition, Fleury recognized the role of these biblical stories and images in enlivening the imagination of the learners, thus more effectively engaging them in the learning process. The first edition of Fleury's catechism included pictures that he had drawn in order to further entice the learner.

Fleury, and others like him, attempted to enhance the usefulness of the catechism by addressing to varying degrees its content and structure.[19] Catechists, theologians, and pastoral leaders presented catechisms to be used by specific groups of people at various times. While this sensitivity to pastoral needs is to be applauded, the result was a proliferation of catechisms. In the United States alone, over a dozen new catechisms appeared between 1800 and 1850, written or officially approved by a local bishop.[20] These were in addition to the many catechisms that immigrants brought with them from their native countries. This expansion in the number of catechisms was one of the strong motivating factors in the call that surfaced in the mid-1800s for a universal catechism, a call that came to the fore at the First Vatican Council (1869).

UNIVERSAL CATECHISM: THE FIRST VATICAN COUNCIL

The historical milieu that gave rise to Pope Pius IX calling for a Church council is complex. A series of dynamics contributed to the situation to which the Church responded defensively. Under the influence of the

Enlightenment and the subsequent rise of Rationalism, the foundation of the Christian tradition was threatened. The notion of divine revelation that had stood secure during the Reformation was now challenged and needed to be defined anew in light of philosophical developments. At the same time, on the political front, the papal states, which occupied a substantial part of northern Italy, were lost to the papacy in the process of the reunification of Italy. By 1860 the papal states were virtually captive; by 1870, the pope's territory had been reduced to a small bit of land over which he was sovereign. It is possible to read subsequent Church events as Pius IX's attempt to gain in ecclesial authority and prestige that which he had lost in land and governance. This forms the context for Vatican I, which was held in 1869 and 1870.

While Vatican I is better known for its decree on infallibility, a review of the council's proceedings indicates that the second most hotly contested topic was the need for a universal catechism.[21] The schema for the catechism, which had been circulated prior to the council's opening, and the subsequent discussion on the council floor made clear that what was being proposed was a "small" catechism, that is, one that was to be placed in the hands of learners. It is also clear that the proponents of the catechism envisioned use of the text made mandatory worldwide.

A number of significant issues came to the fore in the discussion concerning the proposed universal catechism. There were practical considerations. The proliferation of catechisms was seen as even more of a concern in view of people migrating from countryside to city and from Europe to America: the catechism in force in the new setting might well be different from the one left behind. On the other hand, the council discussed the practical challenge of how to implement a universal catechism. There were also questions that were more theoretical in nature. What is the relationship between uniformity and unity? What is the role and responsibility of a local bishop in light of his relationship to the Pope? How do we speak about a common catechism that can appeal to all cultures, all ages, all settings?

Those who supported the catechism and those who opposed it agreed on some central ideas. Members of both groups saw the catechism as a way of enhancing a more centralized notion of the Church. Both groups recognized that a call for a universal, small catechism had as one of its aims a uniformity of expression. And members of both groups recognized the catechism as a response/reaction to the challenges that faced the Church on a variety of fronts, challenges that seemed to threaten the role the Church played in society. While the proponents and opponents of the proposed catechism might agree on the outcomes of a universal catechism, they disagreed whether these outcomes were seen as positive or negative for the life of the Church. In many ways, the perspective that supported the call for a universal catechism was also reflected in the support of the decree on infallibility.

The vote of the council approved the proposed catechism by a wide margin.[22] The catechism itself, however, was never written, as the bishops dispersed without having established a plan for implementing the catechism proposal. The call for a universal catechism was sounded regularly over the next several decades, but it was not until the planning stages for Second Vatican Council that the idea of a universal catechism was again given focused attention. Before we proceed to that discussion, it is helpful to turn back to the United States and recognize the way in which the call for a universal catechism was played out on the national level.

NATIONAL CATECHISM: THIRD COUNCIL OF BALTIMORE

From the very first formal meeting of United States bishops in Baltimore in 1829, a recurring theme at these gatherings was the proposal for a catechism to be used throughout the country. Responding to the increasing number of catechisms and the questionable content of some of them, the bishops attempted first to halt their multiplication by insisting on ecclesiastical approval and then sought to replace the numerous versions with a single one on which they could all agree. Both tasks proved hard to accomplish. By the time of the Third Plenary Council in Baltimore in 1884, no progress had been made in selecting or composing a national catechism satisfactory to all.

Encouraged by the call for a universal catechism at Vatican I, the bishops who gathered in Baltimore in 1884 rallied around the idea of a national catechism and, in 1885, one appeared under the title *A Catechism of Christian Doctrine, Prepared and Enjoined by the Order of the Third Plenary Council of Baltimore.*[23] The next year saw the circulation of an abridged edition that reduced the number of questions and answers from 421 to 208.

The reception of the catechism was mixed, with critics questioning both its length and its usefulness in the classroom. Evidence of the dissatisfaction is the fact that in the ten-year period following its publication, at least seven new catechisms appeared with approval granted by the bishops in the dioceses in which they were written or published; by the turn of the century the number had increased to fifteen.[24] Serious attempts to revise the catechism were underway by 1895, but they met with little success. Although the national catechism was again on the agenda of bishops' meetings into the early 1900s, the debate was finally put to rest when rumors of a catechism written by Pope Pius X offered promise of a satisfactory solution. When the pope's catechism appeared in 1905, it was not presented as a universal catechism and did not resolve the problem of the multiplication of catechisms in this country and elsewhere.

During the first half of this century, a number of factors led to the decline in popularity of the "small" catechism. Development of teaching methodology in the secular realm was translated into religious education with the introduction of the graded series, of alternative methods, and of more appealing formats. The influence of those working in the areas of psychology and religion — George Albert Coe and John Dewey, for example — led to an increased attentiveness to the learners' needs and a move away from the question-and-answer format. The rise of publishing houses that catered to the needs of religious education broadened the offerings for those responsible for catechesis. While various versions and editions of the "Baltimore Catechism" continued to appear, the alternative textbooks were gaining in popularity.[25]

FROM CATECHISM TO DIRECTORY: THE SECOND VATICAN COUNCIL

While the "small" catechism was being superseded by other types of texts, the question of a universal catechism again surfaced in the context of Vatican II. When those planning the council gathered to set forth themes to be explored, the first step was to reflect back on Vatican I in order to discover topics that had been left unfinished by that council. One of the more obvious topics was the proposal for a universal catechism. While recommendations to compose a universal catechism for children were presented in the council's preparatory stages, subsequent discussions led to the conclusion that a single catechism for the universal Church was simply not viable. By the time the council began its deliberation in October 1962, the recommendation was not for a catechism but for a catechetical directory.[26]

The decision to shift from a universal catechism to a catechetical directory is significant. Behind it is the recognition that a small catechism suitable for the whole Church is neither feasible nor, perhaps, even desirable. More importantly, the move from catechism to directory represents a shift in the locus of unity in the Church's catechetical endeavor. Where a catechism serves as a touchstone of orthodoxy in a universal Church, the directory serves as a guide for addressing pastoral issues within a pluralistic situation. The catechism, particularly the "small" catechism, is concerned with uniformity; the directory proposes the possibility of unity within diversity.[27]

Following Vatican II, a commission was established to prepare the "General Catechetical Directory" (GCD), which appeared in 1971. Its goal is to give direction and orientation to catechetical theory and methods without imposing uniformity in text or program. In addition to setting out the general parameters of the catechetical endeavor as it comes to expression in the universal Church, the GCD is also to be used as a guide for the creation of national directories. Following that directive, the bishops of the United States Catholic Conference established a commission to prepare a national directory. Writing the national directory, in consultation with catechetical leaders across the United States on the diocesan and parish level, took six years. It was finally approved and appeared under the title *Sharing the Light of Faith: The National Catechetical Directory* (NCD) in 1979.[28]

At the heart of the directory genre is the invitation to a dialogue between Church and culture. It is significant that the first chapter of the NCD explores the cultural and religious characteristics that affect catechesis in the United States. The starting point for exploring the catechetical enterprise is the culture within which that activity comes to expression. This is not to set up a dichotomy between context and content, but to recognize that the gospel comes alive for each generation, for each culture. It is important to be attuned to the setting within which catechesis takes place, not primarily because teaching can be made more effective but because it is within each culture that God's presence is made manifest anew.

With the realities of U.S. culture as a point of entry, the NCD then sets out the central elements of the catechetical enterprise. As a directory, the NCD delineates the principles and guidelines that underpin catechetical theory and practice. As a directory, the NCD proposes a vision that is to guide catechesis in the United States. As a directory, the NCD aims to promote unity without requiring uniformity, harmony without repudiating diversity. While the text was completed in 1979, it has not been replaced by a subsequent directory; it still serves as a fundamental guide to catechesis in the United States.

Where does the *Catechism of the Catholic Church* fit into this conversation? Is it, in fact, contrary to the spirit reflected in the decision of Vatican II to publish a directory rather than a catechism? That moves us to the question of the nature of the catechism as conceived by the participants of the Extraordinary Synod of 1985. What type of catechism were they envisioning — "small" or "large?" What role is this catechism to play in catechetics on the local level? How did that synod understand the dynamics between unity and uniformity, between the role of local bishops and affiliation with Rome, between culture and catechesis? An analysis of the synod's proceedings can give answers to some of these questions.

Notes for Chapter 2

1. Pope John Paul II, "Closing Address" in *Origins* 15 (December 19, 1985) 452. See Chapter 3 for a discussion of the Synod and the call for a catechism that came from that meeting.

2. Gregory of Nyssa, *The Great Catechism* in *A Selected Library of Nicene and Post-Nicene Fathers of the Christian Church*, ed. Philip Schaff, 2nd series, Vol V (New York: Christian Literature Co, 1893) 471–509. Augustine, *Faith Hope and Charity* in *Ancient Christian Writers: The Works of the Fathers in Translation*, no. 3 (Westminster, Md: Newman Bookshop, 1947).

3. For a discussion of these two texts, see Berard Marthaler, "Compendia, Catechism and Apologetics in the Patristic Era." *PACE* 20 (1991) 79–83.

4. Gregory of Nyssa, 473.

5. Ibid.

6. Augustine, n. 4.

7. Ibid.

8. Ibid., n. 6.

9. This list is taken from the content of the manual prepared in the mid-1300s by John Thoresby, archbishop of York. For a discussion of these catechisms or catechetical manual, see Milton McC. Gatch, "The Medieval Church: Basic Christian Education from the Decline of Catechesis to the Rise of the Catechism" in *A Faithful Church: Issues in the History of Catechesis*, John Westerhoff and O.C. Edwards, eds. (Wilton, Conn.: Morehouse-Barlow, 1981) 99–103.

10. For a discussion of this text see Gerard Sloyan, "Religious Education: From Early Christianity to Medieval Times," in *Shaping the Christian Message: Essays in Religious Education*, Gerard S. Sloyan, ed. (New York: Macmillan, 1958) 28–30.

11. Josef Jungmann provides an insightful analysis of the formative role of medieval culture with its feasts and festivals, its plays and processions. See "Religious Education in Late Medieval Times," in *Shaping the Christian Message*, 38–62.

12. The origin of Luther's catechism is briefly described in the introduction to the "Large Catechism," trans. Robert H. Fischer (Philadelphia: Fortress Press, 1959) 1–2.

13. Ibid., 7.

14. For a discussion of the contribution of Peter Canisius to the development of catechisms, see Berard L. Marthaler, "Catechesis Goes to School: The Catechism of St. Peter Canisius," *PACE* 20 (1991) 201-205. A discussion of the various Catholic catechisms of this period can be found in Mary Charles Bryce, "Evolution of Catechesis from the Catholic Reformation to the Present," in *A Faithful Church*, 205-216.

15. Luther, *Large Catechism*, 7.

16. The edition translated by McHugh and Callan contains an introduction that sets out a brief history of the Council's discussion of the catechism and the process by which the catechism was produced as well as the translations and variations that derived from it. See *Catechism of the Council of Trent*, trans. John A. McHugh and Charles C. Callan (New York: Wager, 1923) xxiii-xxxvii. A helpful discussion of the composition, structure and importance of the Roman Catechism can be found in Berard L. Marthaler, "The Catechism of the Council of Trent," *PACE* 20 (1991) 117-121.

17. *Catechism of the Council of Trent*, 5.

18. Ibid., 73.

19. For a more detailed discussion of Fleury's catechism, see Berard Marthaler, "The Use and Misuse of Catechisms: An Early Critique," *PACE* 22 (January 1993) 3-7. Mary Charles Bryce places Fleury in the context of other catechetical developments in "Evolution of Catechesis from the Catholic Reformation to the Present" in *A Faithful Church*, 216-218.

20. For a discussion of the multiplication of "official" catechisms in the United States, see Mary Charles Bryce, *Pride of Place: The Role of the Bishops in the Development of Catechesis in the United States* (Washington, D.C.: The Catholic University of America Press, 1984) 27-62.

21. Ibid., 78.

22. Ibid., 84.

23. For a detailed discussion of the evolution of this catechism, as well as the general discussion concerning a national catechism in the United States, see Bryce, *Pride of Place*, 87-97.

24. Ibid., 95.

25. For a discussion of the history of developments in catechesis during this period see Kenneth R. Barker, *Religious Education, Catechesis and Freedom* (Birmingham, Ala.: Religious Education Press, 1981) 25-62.

26. An extensive summary of the evolution of the proposal for the *General Catechetical Directory* is clearly presented in Berard Marthaler, "Introduction: The Genesis and Genius of the *General Catechetical Directory*" in *Catechetics in Context* (Huntington, Ind.: Our Sunday Visitor, 1973) xvi-xxx.

27. For an interesting discussion of the evolution of the call for uniformity in catechesis from Vatican I to Vatican II, see Michael Donnellan, "Bishops and Uniformity in Religious Education," *The Living Light* 10 (1973) 237-248.

28. For an analysis of the process used in writing the directory and a summary of the early evaluation of the NCD, see Mary Charles Bryce, "Sharing the Light of Faith: Catechetical Threshold for the U.S. Church" in Warren's *Sourcebook*, 261-274. Also helpful in this context is Ann Marie Mongovan, *Signs of Catechesis* (New York: Paulist Press, 1979).

CHAPTER 3

Synod of 1985: Toward "a Catechism or Compendium of all Catholic Doctrine"

> As regards the valuable suggestions which have emerged during this synod I wish to underline some: The desire expressed to prepare a compendium or catechism of all Catholic doctrine to serve as a point of reference for catechisms or compendia on this theme in all the particular churches; this desire responds to a real need both of the universal Church and of the particular churches.[1]

The *Catechism of the Catholic Church* stands in a long tradition of texts written with some specific intention of presenting a systematic exposition of core doctrine with an aim of facilitating or enhancing catechesis. At various times and for various reasons, attempts have been made to give expression to the elements of Catholic teaching that shape the Roman Catholic Church's perspective on God, on human beings, and on the relationship that exists between them. Continuing in that practice, the *Catechism of the Catholic Church* is presented as

> . . . an organic synthesis of the essential and fundamental contents of Catholic doctrine, as regards both faith and morals, in the light of the Second Vatican Council and the whole of the Church's Tradition (CCC 11).

As we approach the reading of the catechism, we bring with us the understandings and insights drawn from the discussion of the history of catechisms. Two elements of that history are of particular significance here: the context out of which catechisms arose and the function they served. As indicated in the last chapter, the preparation of each catechism took place within a specific historical context to which the catechism was attempting to respond. The call for universal catechisms has been regularly linked with times of conflict or of transition and change: the Reformation, widespread emigration to the Americas with the establishment of fresh expressions of Church in the "New World," and the rise of modernism. These similar social / cultural / ecclesial contexts of the catechisms also point to the catechisms' function. They have served as a basis of unity and standard of orthodoxy. They have been a means of defining more clearly the self-understanding or self-identity of the Church, often in opposition to the positions or perspectives maintained by others.

As we approach our reading of the *Catechism of the Catholic Church*, it is important to examine the immediate context within which this universal catechism was proposed and prepared. Exploring the conversations that gave shape to the proposal and, ultimately, to the preparation of the catechism provides insights into some of the issues at the heart of such an undertaking. From this we also gain some direction in establishing an appropriate methodology for reading and for conveying the meaning of *Catechism*.

As indicated at the end of the previous chapter, discussions about a universal catechism have surfaced repeatedly in the years following Vatican II. But the immediate impetus for drafting the *Catechism of the Catholic Church* is rooted in the Extraordinary Synod of Bishops held November 25 — December 8, 1985.

Called by Pope John Paul II on January 25, 1985, the synod marked the twentieth anniversary of the closing of the Second Vatican Council. As outlined by John Paul II, the synod's aims were:

> To revive in some way the extraordinary atmosphere of ecclesial communion which characterized that ecumenical assembly . . .
>
> To exchange and deepen experiences and information concerning the application of the council at the level of the universal church and the particular church;
>
> To favor further deepening and constant engrafting of [the] Vatican Council onto the church's life, also in the light of the new requirements.[2]

The stated aims of the synod notwithstanding, some early discussions expressed concern about the intended outcome of the synod. The suddenness with which it was announced raised questions regarding the process used in deciding to call the synod; the short time between the announcement and its beginning seemed to preclude the kind of broad consultation necessary for a meeting of this scope. In addition, the set of thirteen questions sent from the Vatican Synod Secretariat to bishops' conferences around the world as part of the preparation for the November meeting raised further concern.[3]

The bishops were asked to respond to a series of four general questions and nine particular questions, all of which focused on four basic themes: the way in which the teachings of Vatican II had been disseminated and implemented, the benefits derived from the council, the errors or abuses in interpretation and application that had arisen, and new needs to be addressed in order for the Church to continue to further the council's vision. In some of the particular questions was an implied presumption that the synod would disclose significant limitations or errors in interpretation and reception of Vatican II.[4] Concerns about the implications of the questions asked, as well as the issues of timing and the decision process, contributed to a less than positive and less than hopeful anticipation of the synod's deliberation. And regardless of later evaluations of the synod, these early suspicions provided one dimension of the context within which synod discussions of a catechism were received in some circles.

THE CALL FOR A CATECHISM IN CONTEXT

The final report of the synod makes clear that a diverse collection of topics were explored during the thirteen-day meeting.[5] Of particular interest to us are three themes which surfaced in various ways and which form the context within which the catechism was proposed. The first of these focuses on catechesis and concerns about the way in which catechesis takes place, particularly in terms of the teachings of Vatican II. The other two themes that bear upon the discussion of a catechism are the continuing conversations about the meaning and means of inculturation and, connected to this, the relationship between the universal and particular church. As we saw in the last chapter, these three topics — catechesis, enculturation, and the relationship between the universal and particular churches — often arise in concert with the suggestion for a universal catechism.

We can examine the deliberations of the synod from four consecutive positions: (1) preparatory statements from the various bishops conferences that reflect each conference's response to the questions posed by the Vatican prior to the synod; (2) the opening report by Cardinal Godfried Danneels, the recording secretary for the synod, designed to summarize the conferences' reports and set the tone for the synod; (3) comments, referred to as "interventions," by individual bishops from the synod floor; (4) and the final report of the synod published after the close of the meeting.

On Catechesis

Issues related to catechesis were brought up at every stage of the synod; in each case the developments in catechesis, as well as the areas in need of further attention were highlighted.

The report submitted to the Vatican Synod Secretariat by the National Conference of Catholic Bishops (NCCB) in the United States makes mention of catechesis in responding to three of the four general questions set out in the Vatican questionnaire: the positive outgrowth of Vatican II (general question 2), problems that have arisen in carrying out the letter and spirit of the council (general question 3), and new needs that have emerged (general question 4).[6]

In discussing the positive expressions of the council, two developments related to catechesis are mentioned: the "proliferation of non-school catechetical programs for various audiences and age levels" and the role that catechesis plays in furthering the understanding of the social justice dimension of the Church's moral teaching (II, B, 6 and 7). Of a more problematic nature has been the struggle to find the appropriate balance between "content" and "experience," and the continuing need for parents to be more involved in the faith formation of the children. Issues related to conscience formation are also discussed in this context (III, A, 6).

Similar concerns are included in the NCCB statement pertaining to new needs that have emerged in the years following the council (general question 4). "New Educational Efforts" is the first heading under which the "new needs" are discussed. First among these education efforts is the need to convey more effectively "the normative character of the church's teaching, the continuity between Vatican II and the preconciliar Church, and the council's grounding in — and, in some areas, reappropriation of — the Catholic tradition" (IV, 1). Focus then turns to the importance of giving further attention to issues of morality, including the role and formation of conscience, sexual morality, and bioethical concerns. Following the discussion of these two areas, the section addressing new educational efforts concludes with the observation that new tools are needed in this endeavor. "Suggestions include a universal catechism of Vatican II, authorized summaries of the council documents written in simple language and audiovisual popularization" (IV, 1).

The opening report to the synod by Cardinal Danneels makes clear that the U.S. bishops were not alone in their concerns about catechesis and their suggestion for a catechism. Within Danneels' report one finds the two-point rationale for the composition of a universal catechism: first, concerns about the normative and lasting character of ecclesial teaching within the context of the Vatican II Church and, second, concerns about morality and conscience formation.

Danneels' opening address to the synod was intended to synthesize the reports from the national conferences and to set the tone for the synod's deliberations. Issues related to catechesis appear in the Danneels' summary of both the positive and negative elements of the national reports. Listed as a positive point is the general renewal of catechesis. In attempting to synthesize the negative points in the national evaluations, Danneels echoes those concerns raised by Malone in the U.S. bishops' report. Danneels writes:

> In some countries there are problems with the integrity and organic structure of catechesis. The gravest problem seems to be in the area of the relationship between morals and the magisterium of the church. . . . A clarification is needed regarding the relationship between objective truth and freedom of conscience.[7]

It is in this context that Danneels makes reference to the request made by some episcopal conference for a "catechism which would provide for the needs of the Church in our epoch after Vatican II, just as the Roman Catechism had provided for the needs of the Church after the Council of Trent."[8] At the conclusion of the report, Danneels also mentions the need for the "information concerning the council to be disseminated through the means of social communication."[9]

Since this synod had no "working paper," Danneels' address served to give focus to the subsequent proceedings. It is not surprising, then, that some of the issues he raised are also discussed in the written and oral interventions and in the language-group meetings. A review of the summaries of the interventions reported in *L'Osservatore Romano* indicates that over half the interventions said something about catechesis, often noting progress in this field.[10]

Among the first on the synod floor to advocate the drafting of a universal catechism was Bernard Law, cardinal-archbishop of Boston. Within the synod, further conversation concerning the catechism took place in the various small language groups. It was here that the desire for a catechism or compendium reflective of Vatican II and designed as a reference work for those involved in catechesis came into focus.[11] Reports from six of the nine language groups recommended the compilation of a catechism.

The final report, drafted by Danneels as recording secretary, was designed to reflect both the topics and tone of the synod proceedings, including both the interventions and various language-groups' discussions. Basically positive and hopeful, the report is divided into two sections, the first exploring the central theme and goal of the synod and the second examining the particular topics explored during the synod. Issues related to catechesis are raised in both sections.

In addressing one of the central themes of the synod, that of furthering the process of implementing the council's vision, the first part of the final report observes:[12]

> There has been full consensus among us regarding the need to further promote the knowledge and application of the council, both in its letter and in its spirit (I, 2).

It later states that the synod recognized that "conciliar doctrines must be proposed in a suitable and continued way" in all areas of ecclesial life, including the catechesis of adults (I, 6).

In the second part of the report, which sets out the particular themes of the synod, a more explicit discussion of catechesis appears in the section entitled "Sources of Life for the Church." Catechesis is seen as a central element both in facilitating full participation in the liturgical life of the Church and in conveying more clearly the word of God as expressed in Scripture, tradition, and magisterium (II, B, a-4 and b-2). It is in the context of this second dimension that reference to a catechism is made.

> Very many have expressed the desire that a catechism or compendium of all Catholic doctrine regarding both faith and morals be composed that it might be, as it were, a point of reference for the catechisms or compendiums that are prepared in the various regions. The presentation of doctrine must be biblical and liturgical. It must be sound doctrine suited to the present life of Christians (II, B, 1-4).

The significance of the recommendation for a universal catechism was made clear at the conclusion of the synod. The closing address by Pope John Paul II cites three "valuable suggestions which have emerged during the synod." The first of these is

> . . . the desire expressed to prepare a compendium or catechism of all Catholic doctrine to serve as a point of reference for catechisms or compendia on this theme in all the particular churches; this

desire responds to a real need both of the universal church and
of the particular churches.[13]

By way of summary then, the issues related to catechesis that surfaced at the synod revolve around a number of central themes: the
need to set out more clearly the teaching of Vatican II, the importance
of a systematic presentation of the Church's teaching, and concerns
relating to morality and conscience formation. It is in the context of
these three themes that the recommendation of a "catechism or compendium of all Catholic doctrine" is situated.

Issues of Inculturation

Before exploring more carefully the nature of the catechism proposed
by the synod, there are two other interrelated themes central to the
synod's deliberation that deserve brief mention here: the understanding of inculturation that has evolved in the Church since the council
and questions related to the relationship between the universal and
the particular churches. Both of these issues have significance in post-
synod discussions of the catechism.

An analysis of the make-up of the synod membership gives sufficient indication that the theme of inculturation would be present in
synod deliberations. Although different methods of counting participants yield differing results, it is clear that over 70 percent of the
bishops' conferences represented were from non-Western countries.[14]

Two quotes might most clearly set out the central dimensions of the
conversation on inculturation. The first is from an intervention by one
of the bishops from Africa. Bishop Sanon of Burkina Faso and Niger
spoke to the assembled synod:

> If, therefore, in the past the encounter between "the Gospel and
> Western culture" gave good results in the doctrinal, dogmatic,
> pastoral, catechetical, liturgical, and other fields, one cannot, how-
> ever, today resolve problems by ignoring cultural data proper to
> the young Churches, still less by despising them, and above all
> by ignoring them. . . . Therefore, one must admit the capital im-
> portance of the problem in inculturation, and on the other hand,
> give a certain trust to the local hierarchy in the field of liturgy and
> sacraments, and hope that at the level of theological thought the
> Churches of the Third World may pass from enjoying and using
> to make their own effective contribution.[15]

The promise of inculturation is set out by Sanon: in the process of taking into their own culture the reality of the gospel and of giving expression to it through liturgy, sacraments, and pastoral action appropriate to their own milieu, the churches of the Third World will not only prosper in faith themselves but will ultimately make a contribution to the theological thought of the whole Church. For this to happen, Sanon argues, the experience of the Third World churches must be acknowledged and respected, and the leadership must be trusted as they endeavor to give expression of the gospel in a cultural context different from that of the Western churches.

That inculturation was a topic of some discussion at the synod is made evident by its presence in Danneels' final report. In the context of discussing the Church's mission in the world, the final report includes a section on inculturation.

> Because the Church is communion, which joins diversity and unity in being present throughout the world, it takes from every culture all that it encounters of positive value. Yet inculturation is different from a simple external adaptation because it means the intimate transformation of authentic cultural values through their integration in Christianity in the various human cultures (II, D, 4).

Here the concern is on the unity that must exist among the diversity. Rather than speaking of the local church rooted within a particular culture, Danneels' focus is the universal Church that can draw valuable elements from each culture as though it were outside that culture. Where Sanon speaks of the need to allow the "cultural data of the young churches" to transform liturgical and sacramental practice and ultimately theological thought, Danneels points to the way in which the Church transforms culture.

So, how do we name the issues related to inculturation? To speak of inculturation is to speak of the dynamic relationship between the gospel and cultures. At the point of intersection between contemporary expression of Christianity and a particular expression of human culture, change takes place. The tension — the "problem" of inculturation — can be expressed in the question: Which changes or which changes more? Is the expression of the gospel message to be shaped and altered by cultural forces or are the values and dynamics of culture to be modified by the gospel message? Sanon and Danneels are addressing these questions from different perspectives.

Our intuition and experience say that this dynamic between gospel and culture cannot be fully understood by an either-or question; both

elements of an interchange of this nature are transformed in the relationship. But as the two quotes above make evident, differences in
emphases are present. The interventions by bishops at the synod on
this topic often called for greater freedom of expression within the
local church in order to respond to cultural differences.[16] The final
report, on the other hand, emphasizes the way in which culture and
cultural values are to be transformed in interaction with the gospel.

A few of the central themes of the relationship between inculturation and catechesis are important for our discussion. At the heart of
the discussion is the fundamental question of the task of catechesis.
What is the nature of the relationships between catechesis and a particular culture and between catechesis and expressions of Church teaching? Again, an "either-or" response sets up an unhelpful dichotomy
— catechesis is *either* about transforming Church teaching to fit cultural
expressions *or* about transmitting an established expression of Church
teaching into a specific culture. It is important to keep in balance the
dynamic tension inherent to those relationships.

Collegiality

One final synod theme that merits our attention is that of collegiality.
It is related to this issue of inculturation but shifts the focus to the internal life of the Church. While inculturation is one way of asking about
relationships between Church and culture, collegiality is one way of
asking about the relationship between the universal and particular
churches. At the heart of the discussion of collegiality is the question:
What is the relationship between the leaders of the universal Church,
expressed primarily through the pope and curia, and the local church,
represented by individual bishops and their national conferences?
Within that are more specific questions: What is the role and authority
of a synod? What is the function and authority of the national conferences of bishops and the statements and documents that come from
them? How are statements from various curial offices to be interpreted;
what is their authority?

One of the significant principles of ecclesiology that came into focus
during Vatican II is that the Church is both universal and local. This
is a departure from the preconciliar notion that the Church is fundamentally understood in universal terms, with each diocese being perceived as an administrative subdivision. After discussing at length the

role of the bishop in his own dioceses, the collegial unity among the bishops, and their relationship with the pope, *Lumen Gentium* (LG) states:

> This Church of Jesus Christ is really present in all legitimately organized local groups of the faithful, which, insofar as they are united to their pastors, are also quite appropriately called Churches in the New Testament. For these are, in fact, in their own localities, the new people called by God, in the power of the Holy Spirit and as a result of full conviction (LG 26).

Within this plurality of churches, unity is established through the collegial unity of the bishops on the regional and national level and, ultimately, on the universal level with the pope as the primary bishop. It is here that the dynamics and significance of collegiality comes into play.[17]

The initial report from Danneels makes clear that this theme was raised by a number of bishops' conferences.

> There remain problems to be resolved: for example, the relationship between the universal and particular churches, the promotion of collegiality, the theological status of the episcopal conferences (this point is often insisted upon), a desire to improve relations with the Roman Curia.[18]

Like the discussion of inculturation, this issue can be presented from two different perspectives: the role of bishops and bishops conferences in having jurisdiction over the local church, on the one hand, and the role of the pope and curial officer in maintaining a universal perspective on the other. But this expression of the debate highlights only the structural or juridical elements of the issue. And while those elements are important, at the heart of the conversation are different perspectives on how best to "be Church" in an ecclesial institution and a world marked by plurality. Questions of the relationship between unity and uniformity, between local expressions and universal principles, are paramount. And for our conversation, the question of the role of a catechism in facilitating these relationships is central.

So, how has the walk through the 1985 synod's deliberation contributed to our understanding of the catechism? First, it is clear that conversations about the catechism are rooted in the broader question of the role and process of catechesis. Second, leading to the recommendation of the catechism was a central concern that the teachings of Vatican II be more clearly and firmly promulgated within the Church. This includes an emphasis on the consistent and normative nature of Vatican II teaching. The synod discussions regularly returned to the concern that the tendency of catechesis to highlight all that has changed since the council misses the point that the council's teachings are in continuity with the past. Finally, review of the synod conversations indicates that the process of communicating the council's teaching is shaped in some way by the reality of pluralism in the Church and in the world. There, the discussion of inculturation and collegiality influence the way in which the proposal for a catechism is understood. These elements contributed to the synod consensus that a universal catechism is needed.

But what exactly was being recommended in these synod proceedings concerning the nature of the catechism? What role was the catechism to serve in the life of the Church? That is the next topic to explore.

THE NATURE OF THE "CATECHISM OF THE CATHOLIC CHURCH"

Was there an immediate recognition of the significance of the proposal for a universal catechism? Or did the idea of a catechism simply seem to be one of the easier and more concrete ideas to write about and talk about? Whatever the cause, the proposed catechism received a good deal of attention in the days during and following the synod. After the immediate reaction subsided, the more challenging task of examining the nature and significance of the proposal began. With the perspective of time and subsequent discussion, we can here set out with some clarity the properties of the catechism proposed at the synod.

What can we say about the nature of the catechism? The first point that is clear is that this catechism is designed to be a "large catechism." In the previous chapter's examination of the history of catechisms, a distinction was made between the "large catechism" and the "small catechism" that was designed for use directly in instruction. Whether planned for children or adults, the small catechism conveyed the teachings of the Church in small, manageable segments, often in a length and cadence appropriate for memorization. Most often, these small catechisms are set out in what we think of as a classic catechism model:

the question-and-answer format. The large catechism, on the other hand, was designed as a resource or reference tool for the person giving instruction and not as a direct tool of instruction. Here the focus is on providing a clear, organized presentation of Church teaching in a way accessible to catechetical leaders; in our history this has most often been the clergy. As we saw in the last chapter, the large catechisms of the past were generally not in question-and-answer format but consisted of short treatises on specific topics often organized around the themes of Creed, sacrament, commandment, and prayer. The clearest example of this type of catechism is the Roman Catechism from the Council of Trent. And it is to this catechism that those at the 1985 synod appealed: Danneels' initial report to the synod spoke of the desire for a catechism that responds to the post-Vatican II Church "just as the Roman Catechism had provided for the needs of the Church after the Council of Trent."[19]

Defining this as a large catechism also makes clear the audience for which the catechism is intended: not for learners, either adults or children, but for catechetical leaders. In his 1987 report on the progress of the pontifical commission established to develop the catechism, Joseph Ratzinger, the cardinal who heads the commission, said:

> In regards to those for whom it is destined, the catechism is directed to those who have the task of composing and / or approving the national and/or diocesan catechisms. It is destined, therefore, especially for the bishops, insofar as they are doctors of the faith. . . .[20]

William Levada, archbishop of Portland and a member of the writing committee, clarifies this a bit further in an address that he gave to a gathering of catechetical publishers. He made clear in that presentation that the intended audience is all those involved in "preparation of suitable catechetical materials for the needs of the various people to whom they minister."[21] The catechism's constituencies, then, are catechists, publishers, and priests as well as bishops. In this sense, Levada argues, it is not a universal catechism — a book designed to be put into the hands of every Catholic — but a catechism for the universal Church.

It is in light of the projected audience that we can focus on the actual intention or goal of the proposed catechism. As we have already seen, the reports from the 1985 synod point to aspects of the catechism's goal: the catechism is to serve as a "clear articulation of the

Church's faith'' in order to be a ''point of reference for the catechisms or compendiums that are prepared in the various regions.'' Post-synod conversations have made evident that the catechism needs to be situated within the broader context of catechesis.

Two points made by John Paul II in his address to the members of the pontifical commission charged with developing the catechism are important to this conversation. First, he was clear in saying that the catechism is not catechesis but only an instrument within this larger endeavor.

> In fact, while the catechism is a compendium of the doctrine of the church, catechesis . . . transmits this doctrine — with methods adapted to the age — so that the Christian truth may become, with the grace of the Holy Spirit, the life of the believers.[22]

Catechesis is concerned with fostering mature faith in the individual and the community; the catechism serves as a resource for that task. The catechist and the formative community of faith serve as the primary medium of catechesis within a particular Church context; the catechism is a resource in support of that activity. Secondly, John Paul takes care to point out that this catechism is not

> . . . a substitute for diocesan or national catechisms, but as a ''point of reference'' for them. It is not meant to be therefore, an instrument of flat ''uniformity,'' but an important aid to guarantee the ''unity in the faith'' that is an essential dimension of that unity of the church. . . .[23]

In the address cited earlier, Levada developed the same point when he said that the catechism was to serve as a point of reference

> . . . by which any catechetical material can be judged for the soundness and comprehensiveness of its approach. As a result, it will supply a measure, ''canon'' or rule, that has been lacking in contemporary catechetics in regard to the content of catechesis.[24]

As a resource for those preparing catechetical materials — programs, textbooks, audio-visuals, etc. — the catechism serves a source of unity, a role that we recognized in the last chapter has been characteristic of catechisms in the past. But the present catechism makes no claim to serve as ground of uniformity in expression or as basis for defining the way catechesis is to take place.

THE CATECHISM: REGRESSING OR PROGRESSING

It seems that we now can return to the question raised at the conclusion of the last chapter: Is the proposal for a catechism for the whole Church a positive sign of continuing the developments made in catechetics in the past thirty or forty years or a negative sign of retrenchment? In his address to catechetical publishers, Levada expressed the question this way:

> Does the universal catechism represent a useful and even necessary step in the implementation of the renewal called for by the Second Vatican Council or does it mean a "regression" of sorts to Baltimore and Trent?[25]

One perspective to take on this question is to ask another question: Is the decision to prepare the catechism as described by the synod a contradiction to the conclusion reached at Vatican II not to publish a catechism but to proceed with a catechetical directory instead? The short answer is "Not really." In an article analyzing this question at some length, Berard Marthaler argues that this catechism is different from the one proposed and rejected at Vatican II because it is designed not for the learners but for catechetical leaders, particularly bishops. In addition, the catechism presumes both the need for adaptation and the role that the bishops are to play in facilitating that.[26]

However, one of the characteristics of the catechetical directory that we mentioned in the last chapter is that the source of unity in the Church rests not in a book but in the bishops and their national conferences. It seems to be a valid concern that the implementation of a catechism for the whole Church shifts the conversation back to the presumption that unity rests in shared words and expressions that have universal applicability and meaning rather than in persons rooted within the local church. And those whose concern has been around issues of inculturation remain disquieted by the presumptions behind the catechism that pluralism of expression can be circumscribed by a book that is necessarily reflective of a limited perspective.

As we discussed earlier, a central concern is the relationship between the way in which Church teachings are verbalized and the culture of the local church within which they come to expression. So while those writing the catechism speak of the need for adaptation, the question remains concerning what that adaptation could look like and still be seen as expression of the teaching of the Church as conveyed in the catechism. We recognize adaptation as more than simply translation. Given a catechism designed for the universal Church, what level of adaptation is genuinely possible? While this question has particular significance for the churches of non-Western cultures, it also has meaning as we think about the way in which the content of the catechism is conveyed within the United States Church. A self-consciousness about the distinctive nature of the U.S. Church, situated within a pluralistic culture, is essential to a meaningful reading and adaptation of a catechism designed for the universal Church. Regardless of the positive perspective held by the proponents of the catechism that the focus is on unity rather than uniformity and that adaptation is a presumed aspect of the project, a number of significant issues remain when we look to applying these ideas to the Church today.

Taken at its most hopeful, however, the way in which the catechism was discussed during the synod, and subsequently, provides some context for a balanced application of principles of inculturation and collegiality. The catechism is designed not to run roughshod over the diversity inherent to a Church that is authentically expressed in a variety of cultural contexts. It is from within the particular culture that local bishops and those preparing catechisms and catechetical materials can give expression to the gospel message and the Church's tradition. It is from within the particular culture that the understanding of who God is, of who human beings are, and of the relationship between God and humans as expressed in the catechism can be incarnated anew.

But while each national Church is to give expression to the catechism in a way appropriate to its own place and perspective, the unity still exists. That unity rests not, however, in a written word that is simply translated into a variety of languages. That unity rests in the dynamic force of collegiality expressed most clearly in the relationship among bishops on the regional, national, and universal levels. It is in the interchange among Church leadership and the respectful dialogue that can exist there that unity within a pluralistic context is possible. The catechism serves as an important shared point of reference in that enterprise.

Amid concerns about the task of giving shape to the *Catechism of the Catholic Church*, there has been a concerted effort to make clear that the text is to be a resource for furthering the developments in catechesis in the years since Vatican II, not a harbinger of retrenchment to models and understandings more suitable for former times. Whether this understanding of the *Catechism* is maintained in the process of receiving and using the text is an important concern and requires a deliberate awareness of the significant question: How do catechetical leaders appropriately draw upon the *Catechism* as resource? How do we "read" this text so that it is a source of unity and not one of restrictive uniformity? Is it possible to respect the issues of inculturation and the dominant role of the local church in shaping catechesis and still use the *Catechism* in a meaningful way?

At its best the new catechism is designed to be part of a context within which variety of expression and creativity of method can flourish. How do we read the *Catechism* to allow it to serve that role? That is the challenge we face as we move now to a consideration of the *Catechism of the Catholic Church.*

Notes for Chapter 3

1. Pope John Paul II, "Closing Address" *Origins* 15 (December 19, 1985) 452.

2. *Origins* 14 (February 7, 1985) 555.

3. For a discussion of the reactions of the call for a synod, as well as the "inside story of the Rome Synod" as the subtitle indicates, see Peter Hebblethwaite, *Synod Extraordinary: The Inside Story of the Rome Synod November — December 1985* (New York: Doubleday & Co., 1986). A somewhat different perspective is proposed in a brief address by Archbishop Tomko, General Secretary to the Synod of Bishops. In responding to those who questioned the pope's intention in calling the synod, Tomko proposes that the synod be situated within the broader context of the pope's thoughts about Vatican II, which Tomko implies are fairly positive. *Origins* 14 (March 27, 1985) 622–623.

4. For a discussion of the elements that contributed to this initial reaction and the nature of the responses from the episcopal conferences to the questions sent from the synod's secretary, see Alberto Melloni, "After the Council and the Episcopal Conferences: The Responses," in *The Synod of 1985 - An Evaluation, Concilium* 188, Giuseppe Alberigo and James Provost, eds. (Edinburgh: T & T Clark, 1986).

5. The report is titled "The Church, in the Word of God, Celebrates the Mystery of Christ for the Salvation of the World," and was drafted by Cardinal Godfried Danneels, the synod's recording secretary. The English translation appeared in *Origins* 15 (December 19, 1985) 440–450.

6. All citations are to the report as printed in *Origins* 15 (September 26, 1985) 225–233.

7. The English language summary of Danneels' report, *Origins* 15 (December 12, 1985) 428.

8. Taken from Danneels' report as quoted by Gerard O'Connell, "The 1985 Extraordinary Synod of Bishops - III: Statements of the Synod Fathers" *Month* 19 (April 1986) 128.

9. *Origins* 15 (December 12, 1985) 429.

10. Berard Marthaler, "The Synod and the Catechism," in *The Synod of 1985: An Evaluation*, 96.

11. For a brief summary of the discussions by language groups, see Berard Marthaler, "The Synod and the Catechism," 96–97.

12. All citations to the Final Report are taken from the translation of the text as it appeared in *Origins* 15 (December 19, 1985) 444–450.

13. *Origins* 15 (December 19, 1985) 452.

14. Jan Kerkhofs, "The Members of the Synod," in *Synod 1985: An Evaluation*, 48–51.

15. Quoted in Gerard O'Connell, "Statements of the Synod Fathers," *Month* 19 (April 1986) 127.

16. Joseph Komonchak, "The Theological Debate," in *Synod 1985: An Evaluation*, 58–59.

17. In an interesting article on the ten basic principles that guide the reforms of Vatican II, Avery Dulles discusses collegiality. When situated within the context of the other principles, the significance of collegiality becomes clear. See "Vatican II Reform: The Basic Principles" in *The Catholic Faith: A Reader*, Lawrence Cunningham, ed. (New York: Paulist Press, 1988) 53–55.

18. *Origins* 15 (December 12, 1985) 429.

19. Taken from Danneels' initial report as quoted by Gerard O'Connell, "The 1985 Extraordinary Synod of Bishops-III: Statements of the Synod Fathers," 128.

20. Joseph Ratzinger, "Toward a Universal Catechism or Compendium of Doctrine." *Origins* 17 (November 5, 1987) 381.

21. "Catechism for the Universal Church: An Overview." *Origins* 18 (March 8, 1990) 650.

22. "Preparing the New Catechism or Compendium of Catholic Doctrine." *Origins* 16 (December 4, 1986) 487.

23. Ibid.

24. Levada, "Catechism for the Universal Church," 650.

25. Levada, 647.

26. Berard Marthaler, "Catechetical Directory or Catechism? Une question malposée," in *Religious Education and the Future*, Dermot Lane, ed. (New York: Paulist, 1986) 68–70.

PART II
Opening the Catechism

OVERVIEW

The approval of the *Catechism of the Catholic Church* by Pope John Paul II in June of 1992 and its subsequent publication in English in 1994 moves the issues discussed in Part I of this text from the theoretical to the practical. Now that we have the *Catechism*, what do we do with it?

In Part II we open the *Catechism* and begin the process of examining its content. Each of the following essays probes one of the parts of the *Catechism*, setting out the foundational themes that give direction to the part's discussion of specific teachings related to the Creed, sacraments, moral life, and prayer. In addition to summarizing the thrust of a part's content, each essay also presents theological concepts or understandings that are presumed in the text but not always clearly explicated. For example, having a clear understanding of the document from Vatican II that gives direction to a particular position will assist the reader in understanding the significance of the discussion. By highlighting both the strengths and weaknesses of each part, the following chapters provide readers with a point of entry for their own discriminating reading of the text. Extensive bibliographical information is included with each of the following chapters; readers are invited to recognize the sources for the theological positions presented in these chapters and to enter into the multifaceted dialogue that exists between the text of the catechism and the thoughts of contemporary theological discourse, between the theological presentation and their own experiences as people of faith, and between the world of theology and that of catechesis.

EVOLUTION OF THE "CATECHISM OF THE CATHOLIC CHURCH"

The previous chapter set out in some detail the context within which the proposal for a universal catechism developed. A look at the synod's discussion of such topics as catechesis, inculturation, and the relationship between the local and universal Church shed light on the theoretical circumstances surrounding the recommendation.

The synod closed in December 1985 with a fairly united call for the preparation of a catechism: both the final report and the pope's closing address specify that one of the key recommendations to come from the synod is for the composition of a catechism. In July 1986 John Paul II established a commission of cardinals and bishops with the responsibility for preparing a draft of the catechism for the universal Church. Members on this commission from the United States were Cardinal William Baum, Prefect for Congregation for Catholic Education, and Cardinal Bernard Law of Boston. The commission established a group of forty consultors from around the world, including Bishop Donald Wuerl of Pittsburgh and Father Francis Kelly of the U.S. Catholic Conference. In addition, seven bishops were asked to serve on the writing committee and prepare the first draft with Dominican Christopher von Schonborn as the editorial secretary of the committee; Archbishop William Levada from Portland, Oregon, was the sole American on this committee.[1]

In November 1989 the draft titled "Catechism for the Universal Church" was sent to bishops around the world. Bishops were directed to evaluate the text and make specific recommendations for its emendation. The "Explanatory Notes" that accompanied the draft indicated that only those recommendations that included specific wording for revising the text would be taken into consideration. This was a daunting task when one considered that the text numbered 434 single-spaced pages and the period allowed for consultation was about five months. Although some confusion concerning the designation *sub secreto* that appeared on most pages of the draft led to a delay in the process, many U.S. bishops did consult theologians and catechists in their effort to critique the draft.[2]

While the individual bishops were preparing their comments to be sent to the Commission for the Catechism for the Universal Church, the Ad Hoc Committee on the Catechism of the National Conference of Catholic Bishops (NCCB) prepared a forty-page general commentary on the catechism and submitted that to the Commission as well. In total, over 24,000 suggestions were submitted to the Commission, which set about preparing the text of the catechism.

It should be noted that the bishops were not the only ones responding to the draft. From the perspective of catechesis, the National Conference of Diocesan Directors of Religious Education (NCDD) prepared a statement evaluating the text and sent it to diocesan catechetical personnel. In addition to reflection by catechetical leadership, theologians also contributed to the conversation concerning the catechism. One of the more significant of these was the symposium held at the Woodstock Center at Georgetown University in January 1990. Sixteen scholars and theologians presented papers examining various parts of the draft catechism. These are assembled in *The Universal Catechism Reader: Reflection and Response.*[3]

A lengthy discussion of the evaluations of the first draft seems pointless at this moment. It is clear that some of the core critiques that were raised from various quarters were attended to in the final text. It is also clear that some elements that were strongly questioned in the draft are still an issue in the *Catechism.* In whatever way the writing committee addressed the various recommendations, the result of their labors — the *Catechism of the Catholic Church* — was approved by Pope John Paul II in June 1992.

The delay in completing and gaining approval for the English translation was troublesome. Long after the French, Spanish, and Italian versions were available, the English version was still being reviewed in Rome. For those in the United States who had been concerned that the catechism would serve as a source of Roman control over American theological thinking and catechetical endeavors, the delay in approving the English version was particularly troublesome. But, delays notwithstanding, the English version was finally approved in February 1994 and was available several months later.

AN ISSUE OF LANGUAGE

The final English translation, prepared by Eric D'Arcy, archbishop of Hobart in Australia, differed significantly from the one that had been circulated among the bishops in English-speaking countries since December 1992. Based on the necessity of a closer correspondence with the original French, the final version includes numerous changes in word-choice and syntax; it is difficult to find more than a handful of paragraphs that have not been changed in some way. D'Arcy himself acknowledges that the earlier version is, in fact, the more readable of the two translations.[4]

The most striking change was the shift away from the use of inclusive language that had been present in the 1992 translation. In the earlier translation, care had been given to use terms such as humanity, human beings, human race, all people. Those preparing the second translation chose to depart from the widely accepted practice in the United States and instead used noninclusive terms such as man, men, brothers, sons. So, for example, the second chapter of Part One, Section One is changed from "God's Initiative" to "God Comes to Meet Man." The first paragraph (#50) of that chapter reads as follows:

> THE 1992 TRANSLATION:
> Although by natural reason we can know God with certainty through creation, there is another order of knowledge, that of divine revelation, which people cannot reach at all by their own power.[5]

> THE FINAL TRANSLATION:
> By natural reason man can know God with certainty, on the basis of his works. But there is another order of knowledge, which man cannot possible arrive at by his own powers: the order of divine Revelation (CCC 50).

In a letter that accompanied the 1992 translations as sent to the bishops of the United States, Cardinal Law of Boston indicated that the translation represented a "moderate approach" to the issue of inclusive language and resulted in a text that "is both readable and useful for the continued work of catechesis which this text is meant to inspire and guide." Clearly, those who revised the translation did not concur with this position.

The effect that the general change in readability of the text and the change in language will have on the usefulness of the *Catechism* in the United States Church is still to be determined. It is certainly an issue that one must bring to the process of reading this text.

THE STRUCTURE OF THE CATECHISM

With the *Catechism* in hand, it is now possible to make some introductory comments about the structure of the text and what that structure says about the nature of the *Catechism* and the way it is to be read. There are three important elements: the topics of the four parts of the *Catechism* and their interrelationship, the relative role of Section One and Section Two of each part, and the role of the "In Brief" sections.

In the prologue to the *Catechism of the Catholic Church*, the writers make clear that the structure of the text is inspired by great traditional catechisms, the Catechism of the Council of Trent (or the Roman Catechism) in particular. As we have seen in our earlier discussion of Reformation catechisms, these texts

> . . . build catechesis on four pillars: the baptismal profession of faith (the Creed), the sacraments of faith, the life of faith (the Commandments), and the prayer of the believer (the Lord's Prayer) — CCC 13.

In the Apostolic Constitution *Fidei Depositum*, which introduces the *Catechism*, Pope John Paul II makes the connection of these pieces clear:

> The four parts are related one to another: the Christian mystery is the object of faith (first part); it is celebrated and communicated in liturgical action (second part); it is present to enlighten and sustain the children of God in their action (third part); it is the basis for our prayer, the privileged expression of which is the Our Father, and it represents the object of our supplication, our praise, and our intercession (fourth part) CCC-FD?

The order of these is not random; it is clear that we first learn of God's love and grace and then respond through lived faith and prayer.

But in addition to the logical unity, there is a unity in foundational notions of who God is, who human beings are, and the relationship that exists between God and humans. At the foundation of each of the parts is a sense of the proactive presence of God as one who creates, initiates, and calls, a presence that is fundamentally Trinitarian. Just as each part begins with the action of God, each part then explores the complementary human response. God's self-revelation evokes a human response of faith; God's saving action and offer of grace evokes a human response of worship and praise; God's call to live in human dignity evokes a response of moral living; God's invitation to relationship evokes a response of prayer.

It is clear that the structure of the *Catechism* invites the reader to recognize the fundamental unity of the Church's teaching around the core belief in God's loving presence expressed most clearly in the saving action of Jesus Christ.

Each part is divided into two sections: Section One examines the theological foundation for a consideration of specific teachings set out in Section Two. For example, Section One of Part One (''The Profession of Faith'') sets out the fundamental understanding of the human being as one who is called by God. It reminds us that God takes the initiative and that faith is our human response to God's call. Only with that in mind do we enter into a discussion, in Section Two, of the articles of the Creed. Section One of Part Two ("The Celebration of the Christian Mystery") first situates the discussion of sacraments within the broader context of the liturgical life of the Church; this becomes the context for examining each of the sacraments separately in Section Two.

Each part begins with the broader theological foundation that sustains the discussion of details. One of the clearest implications of this for our reading of the text is that each part (and ultimately the entire *Catechism*) must be seen as a whole. It is possible to flip through Section Two of any given part and locate the paragraph that gives the "answer" to a specific question. That paragraph, however, read out of context, remains but a partial response that the *Catechism* is able to provide. Situating that "answer" within the context of the theological foundations set out in Section One of any particular part provides a depth of understanding. The "answer" one might find within the *Catechism* is best understood when framed by the discussion of the various dimensions of God's action and human response as explored in Section One of each of the parts.

One further observation on this discussion of the relationship between Section One and Section Two of each of the parts of the catechism: there are places in each of the parts where there seems to be a mismatch or lack of congruence between Section One and Section Two. In setting out the details and digressions of a particular article of the Creed, or sacramental practice, or issue in morality, or phrase in the Lord's Prayer, there are places when the text of Section Two seems to "forget" the broader picture of the proactive presence of God. In these cases the reader has the responsibility to interpret the specifics in light of the more central foundational perspective of the mystery of God's love.

A final point concerning the structure of the catechism rewards consideration: the nature and role of the "In Brief" sections. At the conclusion of each of the *Catechism*'s articles, on average every four or five pages, there is an attempt to summarize the preceding discussion in a series of statements. The *Catechism* describes them this way:

> At the end of each thematic unit, a series of brief texts sum up the essentials of that unit's teaching in condensed formulae. These "In Brief" summaries may suggest to local catechists brief summary formulae that could be memorized (CCC 22).

These do serve to focus the reader's attention on key concepts explored in detail in the text, providing an outline of sorts for the preceding pages. However, some problems exist. There are points in the *Catechism* where the "In Brief" section does not correspond closely to the text. In other places the phrasing of these "In Brief" sections is easily confusing to the reader and does not fairly represent the more nuanced discussion in the text. And, there are places where the tone or emphasis that had been fairly balanced in the text comes down strongly on one side or another of a discussion. By conclusion, then, one must read the "In Brief" sections within the context of the full text and as a summary of the preceding section.

This discussion of some specific problems with the "In Brief" sections raises a more significant issue concerning their use in catechesis. The description of the "In Brief" sections within the *Catechism* itself gives the impression that they could be taken out of the context of the text and used for catechesis and as points to be memorized. While memorization can be a positive element in faith formation, care needs to be taken when the material memorized is not drawn from Scripture, creeds, or traditional prayers of the Church.

The structure of the *Catechism* provides insights for how the text is read. First, the text needs to be read as a whole. Discussions of human response to key ideas about God's presence, particularly in Jesus Christ, run throughout the entire text and form the core around which the other concepts are meaningful.[6]

Second, within each part, Section Two must be read in the context of Section One. The details of specific teachings need always to be situated within the broader conviction of the Christian understanding of God's presence. Finally, the text as structured is not an answer book; it is not first and foremost about specific teachings. It is a presentation of our best attempt to express the mystery of God's love. The opening of the *Catechism* makes clear that it is about our response to God, our response to God's desire to be in relationship with us, our response to the initiative that God has taken to share the divine life with us. It is only in that context that specific teaching and statements of doctrine and Church practice make sense.

Notes for Overview

1. Information for this chronology is culled from William Levada, "Catechism for the Universal Church: An Overview" *Origins* 19 (March 8, 1990) 649.

2. For a brief summary of the process of consultation, see Thomas J. Reese, "Introduction," in *The Universal Catechism Reader: Reflections and Responses,* Thomas Reese, ed. (San Francisco: Harper Collins, 1990) 2–4.

3. For a review of the materials written in response to the call for a universal catechism as well as that written about the draft, see Thomas J. Reese "Bibliographical Survey on the Catechism for the Universal Church," *The Living Light* 27 (Winter 1991) 151–157.

4. For a discussion of the contribution of Eric D'Arcy to the translation process, see Chris McGillion, "Doctoring the Catechism," *The Tablet* 21 May 1994: 624–635.

5. "The Catechism of the Catholic Church" Pro Manuscripto, copy reserved for the bishops. (Vatican City: Libreria Editrice Vaticana, 1992).

6. For a discussion of the way in which hierarchy of truths is given expression in the catechism, see Christopher Schonborn, "Major Themes and Underlying Principles of the *Catechism of the Catholic Church,*" *The Living Light* (Fall 1993) 57–60.

CHAPTER 4

The Profession of Faith

Michael P. Horan

A careful reading of any written work is a rich and risky activity. It invites a variety of interpretations, and with that variety comes the opportunity to generate a wealth of meaning for any text. However, there is the possibility that the variety and diversity of meaning may merely cloud the text rather than illumine it. In order to gain the greatest clarity on the text of the *Catechism of the Catholic Church*, it seems wise to consider the overall structure of each of the four parts, and to refer to those sources, mostly Church documents and movements, that have helped to shape this text.

The focus of this chapter is the first of the four parts that make up the *Catechism* — "The Profession of Faith." Part One is divided into two major sections. Section One, entitled "I Believe — We Believe," establishes general principles for approaching the content of the Christian faith professed in the Creed. Section Two of Part One presents that content by offering an expansion and reflection on the articles of the Apostles' Creed.

In our consideration of Part One, we examine first the overall structure of the part; second, the sources that inform most directly Section One of Part One; and, finally, we explore some areas for further research that might round out the reading and use of the text.

STRUCTURE OF SECTION ONE OF PART ONE

The overall structure of Part One, Section One of the *Catechism* is determined by its fundamental theology of revelation and faith. This is best described as a *dynamic relationship* that exists between a *divine invitation* through revelation and a *human response* in faith. The writers of the *Catechism* are able to illustrate the theological dynamic by both the structure of Section One and the content that the section treats.

The foundation for understanding revelation as invitation-response can be traced back to Vatican II and the theological developments that preceded and supported the council's pronouncements. This understanding of revelation suggests an advance over the descriptions of revelation found in Church documents before the council. The basis for this invitation-response dynamic is the reaffirmation at Vatican II that Scripture reveals a story of salvation for all people in the mystagogy of liturgy.[1] The story of this reaffirmation had roots in the currents of thought found in Catholic theology in the years before Vatican II.

Prior to the council, a renewed interest in historical sources propelled Catholic theologians to study afresh the clues to the life of faith found in the Patristic era of Christianity. An accompanying movement in theology witnessed Catholic theologians trained to analyze the composition of Scripture and various methods of biblical research in order to provide clarity to these sources of the Church's young faith. These insights bore fruit in the council's exhortations to Catholics to return to the sources of faith life found in the liturgy and the Bible. The renewal of liturgy after Vatican II went hand in hand with new gains in knowledge about Scripture, the writing of Scripture, and the communal character of the first churches in their cultural diversity of expression yet fundamental unity of faith.

It may be helpful to review the sources for this invitation-response dynamic found in selected theological insights from Vatican II, as these provide the context in which to view the organizing dynamic in Section One.[2] These same insights form the foundation for the subsequent developments in postconciliar catechetical theory and in the *Catechism of the Catholic Church*.[3] The principal document that aids us in reading Section One of Part One is the Dogmatic Constitution on Divine Revelation, entitled *Dei Verbum* (DV).[4] The title *Dei Verbum,* or *Word of God,* is itself significant, as we will see when we analyze the content of the document.

"DEI VERBUM" IN CONTEXT:
THE INVITATION-RESPONSE DYNAMIC

Many of the sixteen council documents relate directly to the overall theme of Vatican II: The Church's self-identity and internal understanding and functions on the one hand, and the Church's relationship to the worldwide culture and its mission within culture on the other. But quite different from that emphasis, *Dei Verbum* directly treats the topic of revelation and assumes that revelation concerns God's self-disclosure and invitation to humans to acknowledge that we are all in relationship to God. Before there is a Church, and even before there is a revelation in and through Jesus the Christ, there was and remains the human desire for meaning that eventuates for the believer in the discovery that God is already always inviting us to relationship through the human desire itself. *Dei Verbum* affirms the invitation-response dynamic in its content as well as its structure.

Sometimes people think of revelation as the *content* or *message* that God sends in dramatic ways to a few individuals. As presented in *Dei Verbum*, however, revelation is first and foremost God's self-disclosure in a *personal* way to the individual and to the world. This disclosure may occur in a *direct* way, but generally it occurs in *indirect* ways through history and those events in time that carry forward God's message of salvation to humanity. Hence *Dei Verbum* stresses God's disclosure through events like the Exodus from bondage in Egypt to the freedom of the land promised first in covenant to Abraham (DV 3).⁵ The events of Hebrew history are celebrated in liturgies and expounded through homilies as God's Word not only for our ancestors in faith but for contemporary Christians. The theme of freedom from bondage, for example, is not only proper to remembering the Exodus of the Israelites, but it carries deep meaning about liberation from various kinds of oppression. It "reveals" wisdom to victims and oppressors alike. With Christian tradition, *Dei Verbum* insists that the public revelation of Jesus the Christ is an unsurpassable disclosure of the personal and historical dimensions of God's design.⁶

The *Catechism* follows these basic ideas in such a close way that Section One conforms its structure to the outline of *Dei Verbum*.⁷ Like the dogmatic constitution, Part I of the *Catechism* attends first to the nature of revelation itself and then to the transmission of revelation by Scripture and tradition. God reveals through deeds and words (CCC 53), and the classic example of this revelation is the divine plan to save humanity, a plan instituted from the dawn of creation through the history of Israel, a people in covenant with God. The covenant that was breached by the sin of our first parents is rectified by God through the upright figures of the Hebrew testament; Noah, Daniel, and Job are among them (CCC 58). Moses' law and the priestly people of Israel, including the prophets who proclaimed a radical redemption of God's people (CCC 62-64), are joined by "such holy women as Sarah, Rebecca, Rachel, Miriam, Deborah, Hannah, Judith, and Esther" (CCC 64). All these prophets lead toward the "fullness of revelation" found in Jesus Christ (CCC 65-67).[8]

We have briefly reviewed the nature of revelation as God's personal and historical self-disclosure. What is clear from this review is that the conciliar document *Dei Verbum* and the *Catechism* follow the same basic lines of discussion about the nature of revelation. Both documents emphasize the public or communal character of revelation and its indirect disclosure through historical events that are understood by believers to have saving significance. How is that revelation actually handed on from one generation of believers to the next? How does one move from the personal faith claim ("I believe") to the communal transmission of that claim ("We believe")? Let us turn attention to the transmission of revelation as described in the *Catechism* with reference to its source, *Dei Verbum*.

INVITATION FOUND IN SCRIPTURE "AND" TRADITION

Let us consider the questions we have just raised by examining the historical context for a theology of revelation. The achievement of *Dei Verbum* becomes clearer when it is viewed alongside earlier official theologies of revelation.

One achievement of *Dei Verbum* is its emphasis on tradition as a dynamic reality that is inextricably bound to the Scriptures, the sacred Word of the community.[9] This emphasis signals an advance over the earlier conciliar discussion of revelation that took place one hundred years before Vatican II, at the First Vatican Council (1869-70). That council had promulgated a document on revelation entitled *Dei Filius*. In that earlier document from the First Vatican Council revelation was described in relationship to human reason. *Dei Filius* displayed an understanding of revelation as propositional; that is, as communication of divine truths from God which break into the created order and which rely on but surpass human reasoning for their meaning and reception. Here we see the Church's attempt to mediate disputes between those persons who emphasized the importance of faith in receiving revelation on the one hand and those who exalted the role of reason in receiving revelation on the other.

This search to illumine the knowability of revelation was helpful to people of the nineteenth century as they attempted to make sense of the theological disputes of their time. Much of the Church's attention was captured by the philosophical strains of the "Age of Reason," the Enlightenment. The Enlightenment philosophers contributed a definition of knowledge in terms of intellectual apprehension of the object or thing to be known. This definition offered the world a new understanding of reality in empirical (or sensory data) terms. Fueling the Enlightenment definition of knowledge were the scientific discoveries that challenged the receding understandings of reality found in religious cosmologies. Responding defensively, the Church condemned those who dissented from the standard religious understandings of the natural world (e.g., a literal reading of the creation accounts in Genesis 1-3). Vatican I wrestled with the cultural consequences of the Enlightenment[10] and therefore focused on how one comes to *know* anything, including non-empirical knowledge such as revelation. In the face of faith claims about revelation, the council fathers at Vatican I needed to ask how they might *prove* that this revelation is knowable.

In *Dei Verbum* and in the *Catechism* we witness something very different from the theology of revelation found in the document from the First Vatican council. *Dei Verbum* offers a Catholic affirmation of the importance of human experience in the process of understanding and interpreting Scripture. The Vatican II document and the *Catechism* also stress the accompanying need to link Scripture with tradition, in part to inform the interpretation of the writings that stand at the heart of the Christian experience. In this context tradition is understood as that dynamic reality which we witness whenever the perspective of faith and the content which supports that perspective are passed on from one believer to another, and especially from one generation to the next.

Dei Verbum and the *Catechism* sustain long discussions about the relationship between tradition and Scripture in order to describe this divine invitation that Christians call revelation. For if revelation is personal, it is also effected historically, particularly through the history of salvation found in the biblical record of Israel and the young church of disciples. Recognizing that the meaning of the Bible and the early Church documents is not self-evident from a surface reading, the writers of both *Dei Verbum* and the *Catechism* emphasize the analysis of, and appreciation for, the early texts.

REVELATION: HISTORICAL AND COMMUNAL

The writers of the *Catechism* offer us the foundations for what at least one theologian has called the "salvation history model" of revelation.[11] Hence the *Catechism* describes God's invitation as salvation-historical through Israel's struggles and through the ancient mode of "typology" that finds in the "old covenant" the "prefigurations of what [God] accomplished in the fullness of time in the person of his incarnate Son" (CCC 128).[12] More than the typological approach, however, this section of the *Catechism* presents the foundations for understanding the Bible as a document that reveals both the historical Jesus beneath the Gospel stories and the Christ, the object of the disciples' faith proclaimed in those Gospels. This is accomplished by a clear presentation of the historical critical method of analyzing the Scriptures.

The historical critical method of analyzing Scripture is based in the Enlightenment methods of scientific research. First blessed by the official teaching Church in 1943 in *Divino Afflante Spiritu,* this method has uncovered the truth that the writing of the Gospels occurred in three stages: (1) The life and teaching of the historical Jesus, (2) the oral tradition of the disciples who experienced the Lord's resurrection, and (3) the composition of the writings we now call the canon of the New Testament (CCC 126).[13] The *Catechism* indicates that the Gospels result from the fusion of many elements, including the orally communicated stories, some written sources, and the synthesis and reflection of the Church.[14] This three-stage theory is widely accepted both in official Catholic theology and in most mainline Protestant Churches. The insight beneath this theory is that revelation occurs through the tradition as well as in the inspired Word of God that is expressed through the words of Scripture.

Interestingly, the description of revelation found in Section One concludes with the location of Sacred Scripture within the life of the Church, exhorting minsters of the word to appreciate and regard the "study of the sacred page" as the very soul of theology. This echoes a similar call found in the conclusion of *Dei Verbum* (DV 24).

FAITH

If revelation is God's invitation to participate in a dynamic personal relationship in history and community, then faith is humanity's response to the invitation. This brief section of the *Catechism* functions as the bridge between Section One and Section Two of "The Profession of Faith." Section Two is the heart of this part, as it offers the content of faith for which the *Catechism* was written. The sources for the discussion of faith in this section are two: The New Testament letters and the document *Dei Filius* from the First Vatican Council. The model person of faith described in this section is Abraham, and the primary source for the description is the Epistle to the Hebrews, chapter 11. That chapter describes Abraham's trust and obedience.

Here is some background that contextualizes this section of the *Catechism:* Traditionally, theology in the west has distinguished between two notions of faith: faith as *fides qua,* or the activity of trusting or believing anything, and *fides quae,* the object of that trust, or its content. Focusing on the *fides qua,* we might reflect on the *act* of faith, or the *ability* to trust in the goodness of reality, in the word of others, and ultimately in God. If asked why we trust, we might reflect on those experiences and events that constitute the content of our trusting; the person or conviction in whom or in which we believe. So traditional theology has consistently affirmed the necessity of both of these dimensions of faith. Faith as trust, as a risk or as a "leap" in the dark, is an appropriate image in contemporary culture.

This section of the *Catechism* establishes the *fides qua,* or *act* of faith, as the preamble to the major portion of Part One, which is the *fides quae,* or *content* of faith, i.e., the Creed, whose content we will examine in Section Two. Unfortunately, the reader of the *Catechism* will need to supplement the treatment of faith found in the all-too-brief section. Important direction can be found in this brief section, however, as here and elsewhere the *Catechism* functions as the beginning rather than the end of the human drive to understand the activity as well as the content of faith.

SUMMARY

The first section of Part One provides important principles for outlining "the faith" of the Church in the second section. The guiding principles are the Church's understanding of revelation and faith. Clearly the writers of this section focus more on revelation than on faith. In their focus on revelation, the compilers of the *Catechism* wish to show that revelation is a divine invitation that is both deeply personal and fundamentally communal. This invitation carries forward a communal context and eventually an ecclesial affirmation of the faith of all Christians. In their faithfulness to the insights of Vatican II, especially to the articulation about revelation found in the conciliar document *Dei Verbum*, the writers of the *Catechism* adopt a salvation history approach that respects the communal and liturgical character of the story of God's initiative to save Israel and the Church. In adopting this approach, the writers affirm the insights of scientific scholarship on the Bible that would lend meaning to the Word of God. Thus, the writers prepare the way to encounter the God who creates and redeems and sanctifies, through Christ in the Holy Spirit, the God, in Unity and Trinity, in whom we Christians believe. The heart of the matter for Christian belief can be encountered in the Creed, contained in Section Two of the part on "The Profession of Faith."

SECTION TWO OF PART ONE

Section Two of Part One lays out the structure for the review of the entire Creed as the summary of the content of the Christian faith. Interestingly, this section begins with a reiteration of the communal character of faith, a theme that we have seen in the first section of the part: "Whoever says '*I* believe' says 'I pledge myself to what *we* believe' " (CCC 185). The writers of the *Catechism* want to remind us that creeds function as syntheses as well as symbols; that is, they draw together those elements that are the object of faith and they also provide the sign of communion among believers of disparate cultures and backgrounds.

The presentation of the content of faith in the *Catechism* follows the lines of the Apostles' Creed. Frequently in catechesis and in theological analysis of the Creed, writers and preachers point out the Trinitarian structure of the Creed as a way to understand its organic unity. The writers of the *Catechism* follow this pattern, and therefore they begin with the following topics about God as First Person of the Trinity: God as truth in Oneness and Trinity; God as Father and Creator; angels and the world as the created order of the Creator; the creation and fall of the human family; and the necessity of salvation. The final subsection in the discussion of God, and the bridge to the discussion of the Christ, is entitled "You Did Not Abandon Him to the Power of Death." This order of presentation of the content communicates an order for creation and the fall of humans. But it also reestablishes the time-honored logical framework for an argument for the necessity of the incarnation.

CHRISTOLOGY FROM ABOVE

Nearly a millennium has passed since St. Anselm of Canterbury constructed a similar argument in his work entitled *Cur Deus Homo* ("Why God Became Human"). In that work Anselm reasoned that the sin of humanity so dishonored God that honor could be restored only by one obedient servant who, though equal to God, chose to take the part of the disobedient servant, becoming like those who dishonored God. Thus the necessity of the incarnation seemed to be a reasonable as well as gracious reality to the generation of theologians and preachers who first followed Anselm's lead. Anselm used imagery from the feudal social class system in a society that assumed that the dishonor done by a servant toward a lord could not be rectified except by one equal to the greater class. The scene, as Anselm depicted it with his pen and skill, displays the necessity of the incarnation for the salvation of humanity through God's Word enfleshed in Jesus Christ.

The achievement of Anselm's "argument" has been hailed for centuries. But his thinking seems deficient to hearers and readers in a world like ours. Anselm's interests were circumscribed by his culture; that is true of each generation. Yet precisely his interests and bias allowed him to bypass the issue that plagues contemporary society approaching the twenty-first century. Anselm's contemporaries raised questions in the eleventh century about the meaning of the claim that God assumed full humanity. Conversely, our generation is fascinated and frightened by what it means to be human.

Our contemporary generation, shaped first and decisively by the Enlightenment, regards the human as first of all an individual in freedom. This new perspective on the human being has been the object of our fascination and at the same time a contributing factor to our failings. Despite this generation's unsurpassed scientific achievements, the people of the twentieth century have witnessed so much horror that we must approach the question of what it means to exercise human freedom with fear as well as fascination. Two world wars, the Holocaust, the nuclear threat, and an ecological crisis of apocalyptic proportions offer legitimate reasons to be fearful as well as fascinated by the question, since we know well our potential for self-destruction from within and obliteration from without.

Recent theological works on Jesus have responded to the spirit of contemporary times and needs by starting with the examination of Jesus' humanity. This development has two advantages: it responds to the needs of society today, and it offers a forum in which to pursue those questions of biblical scholarship that have been the focus of study since the eighteenth century: a quest to know and encounter the historical Jesus at the core of New Testament faith.

In the face of all this, the *Catechism* does not begin in the manner one might have wished it to begin. Rather than beginning from an examination of humanity, both Jesus' and ours, Chapter Two of Section Two begins with a Christology "from above." The focus within the *Catechism* is the divine nature and role of Jesus the Christ as one sent by God to achieve our salvation. From this perspective, the study of Jesus found in the *Catechism* reaffirms and expands our credal statements, but it does not offer the theological supports for these statements about Jesus. While the writers say more than the articles found in the Creed, they do not illumine the *meaning* of these statements by a creative use of theology. Therefore, catechetical leaders might well review the theology that shapes this document, as well as the Christology that would complement this work. In what follows we will review briefly the basic Christological orientation of the *Catechism*, and consider three related issues that light up current scholarship on Jesus, areas of concern that complement the treatment of Jesus found in the credal section of the catechism.

CHRISTOLOGY IN THE CATECHISM

The organizing idea for the *Catechism*'s discussion of Jesus is found in the Epistle to the Galatians 4:4-5, in which we are reminded that in the fullness of time, God sent the Son, born of a woman and born under the law, so that we might receive adoption as children of God. The introduction of Jesus the Christ is accomplished by an analysis of the titles accorded him. The writers discuss the meanings of "Jesus" and "Christ," as well as "Son of God" and "Lord," in an effort to display the divinity of Christ and the predetermined plan by God for the salvation of the world through Christ. This approach to Christology, often referred to as a "high descending Christology" or a Christology "from above," takes its name from the starting point for examining Jesus Christ as the Word become flesh. This approach is one of the two classic points of departure for understanding Jesus Christ in full humanity and full divinity. The authors employ this high descending Christology without explaining its assumptions or without the complementary approach, known as a "low ascending Christology" or a Christology "from below." Low ascending Christology, that style of Christology which complements its partner, begins the study of Jesus Christ by an historical critical examination of the human Jesus, the person in whom the first disciples come to recognize the anointed one, the Christ. Neither approach is complete in itself, and therefore both are important to the full discussion of the Christian claim about Jesus Christ. Let us turn to the *Catechism's* high descending approach, and then to the complementary approach.

THE WORD MADE FLESH

The *Catechism's* authors expand the assertion of God's plan of salvation by explaining why the Word became flesh and was born in Jesus (CCC 456ff). The reasons are for the reconciliation and atonement for the sin of humanity (CCC 457), for humans' experiential knowledge of God's love for us (CCC 458), and to provide an example of holiness for all people (CCC 459). Moreover, the incarnation of God in Jesus Christ effects the fundamental change in our condition as humans, by making us participants in the divine nature. This final reason is explained by quoting St. Athanasius: "For the Son of God became man so that we might become God" (CCC 460); and St. Thomas Aquinas, who asserted that the Son of God assumed our human nature so that he might make us gods (CCC 460). These quotes illustrate the high descending Christology of the *Catechism* text. They are reflections on the Christology forged by the Church in its reflections, and summarized in the early councils of Nicaea, Chalcedon, and Constantinople. The authors of the *Catechism* review each of these three councils and the false teachings about Jesus Christ's humanity-divinity that each council sought to address.[15]

Following the review of conciliar Christology, the *Catechism's* authors take up a discussion of Mary's predestined role as Virgin Mother of God, the Bearer of the Word made flesh. This discussion is a corollary to the high descending Christology found in the preceding section.

Reviewing the catechesis on Mary, the authors relate Mary's life of faith to the earthly life of Jesus. Interesting and even curious is the treatment of the mysteries of Christ's life, not as they may have been historically, but as they are remembered and celebrated *liturgically*. CCC 522 begins the mysteries as interpreted through Advent and each season of the liturgical year. To summarize: this section does not develop the historical critical findings about the human Jesus that might complement the discussion of the early Church councils and the Christian faith affirmations about Christ. It assumes the posture of a reflection on the story of Jesus Christ found in the Gospels and celebrated in the liturgy. But it does not follow the lines of historical critical analysis of the New Testament that the writers of the *Catechism* reviewed and applauded in Section One of the part on Christian Faith. The result is a Christology that has reflective and homiletic significance. However, more information on the historical Jesus would help catechetical leaders who need to refer to a compendium of faith as Catholic minds currently analyze and articulate that faith. Therefore we turn to some areas for further consideration.

AREAS OF CONCERN IN CHRISTOLOGY

We have already seen that Section One of Part One affirms that biblical research and the historical critical methods of biblical analysis help us to encounter the earthly Jesus who is the Christ. Let us turn to the results of research in those methods used by Catholic scholars in recent years in order to complement the approach and content of Christology found in the *Catechism*. Two representative areas that help to illumine the historical Jesus are, first, the Jewish identity of Jesus and, second, Jesus' commitment to the reign of God. While there are other areas that could be treated in a review of recent findings on the historical Jesus and the fruit of Scripture scholarship, these two cry out for attention in the *Catechism*, and in the pastoral life of the church for which it is a resource.

The Jewishness of Jesus

Recent scholarship on the religious roots of Jesus' teaching have helped Christians to move from previously unexamined assumptions about his place within his faith. For example, it is now well accepted that

Jesus was close to the Pharisee party in his interpretation of the Torah and that there were several interpretations even within Pharisaic Judaism in the first century that represented competing claims about the way to live Torah. Jesus' followers may have needed to distance themselves from the Pharisees of their generation more than Jesus needed to. Thus the Gospels, written after the death-resurrection experience and two generations of oral tradition, cannot be used uncritically to claim Jesus' distance from his contemporaries. This insight has significance not only for professional theologians, but it carries importance for the pastoral life of the Church.

Since Vatican II the relationship between Jews and Christians has received greater official attention. Building upon the council, the Vatican *Guidelines and Suggestions for Implementing the Conciliar Declaration "Nostra Aetate,"* released in January 1975, points out that real dialogue between the two related faiths has scarcely risen to the level of monologue.[16] On the topic of the Jewishness of Jesus, even less has been said. The sin of anti-Semitism among Christians either stems from (at least in part) or is fueled by Christian ignorance about Jesus the Jew. Effective catechesis on this topic will provide the necessary preparation for dialogue on the local level in the workaday world of Christians and Jews. This area of Christological research bears clear implications for the pastoral life of the Church.

Commitment to the Reign of God

Jesus' ministry in the context of his Judaism appears to have been deeply related to an alternative vision of the reign of God as that reign affected the life of Israel. Scholars today note that Jesus' commitment to God's reign translated quite practically in Jesus' life into a preference for the poor and marginalized persons of the society in which he found himself. His treatment of widows and orphans, his regard for the "anawim" or poor persons who tilled the land as daily workers without rights or status, his interactions with women in general displayed a fundamental insight about God's intention to reveal the divine will through humanity, especially in those persons who know suffering and oppression all too intimately.

Perhaps the most helpful tool for interpretation of the Gospels in recent years has come through those theologies that have come to be known as "contextual theologies,"[17] or systems of thought that are deeply related to the practice of Christian faith and the call to create a just society based in the reign of God. In the light of new methods of biblical research, these contextual theologies seek to uncover the goodness of the good news for those who are least likely to receive favor from society. Contemporary scholars concur that Jesus' understanding of the reign of God contained in the Gospels is different from some of his contemporaries, yet it remains within the reach of other Jewish reformers. In the face of this knowledge, Christians can proclaim the goods news to the poor and liberty to captives as the prophet Isaiah first insisted (Isa 61).[18]

Read in the light of the historical critical findings, the parables and miracle narratives provide access to Jesus' understanding of God's reign. The parables and miracles reveal a Jesus on the side of the poor, the "good Samaritans," and the tax collectors who recognized their need for conversion. Indeed the Gospel portrays a Jesus who embraces the very ones whom the civil and religious authorities found wanting. The findings of contextual theologies and their hermeneutical tools coincide with a commitment to praxis, or the activity of faith that reflects on itself and its fidelity to the Gospel portraits of Jesus as the one committed to creating a just society in which God reigns. The ancient Israelites challenged the interpretations of their neighbors by showing that God reigns not only in and through acts of nature but in and through the events of salvation history. Jesus demonstrates God's reigning activity in and through those people on the margins, rather than those at the center, of history. This understanding of Jesus' words and work results directly from the findings of scholars who have been engaged in the methods of biblical research outlined in Section One of Part One. This challenging interpretation of Jesus' ministry continues to spur on the works of justice in our world today.

So we can confidently conclude that this biblical hermeneutics functions not only to enrich theological conversation but has a direct bearing on the pastoral life of the Church. Like the absence of a clear discussion of the Jewish historical Jesus, the lack of attention to the theme of the reign of God amounts to a breach of the *Catechism*'s own principles as established for us in the part's Section One. Therefore, when judged by its own criteria, the treatment of Jesus Christ found in the *Catechism* will demand the supplements and amplification to which the writers refer (CCC 24).[19]

To summarize: The high descending Christology found in Section Two of Part One could have been written before the Second Vatican

Council and without benefit of the findings of the historical critical method of Bible study that has been the glory of mid-twentieth century Catholic theology. By ignoring the findings of the very methods which they report and laud in the first section of Part One, the *Catechism's* writers miss the opportunity to offer both approaches to Christology (i.e. high descending as well as low ascending) and thereby leave to catechetical leaders a task to be pursued independently of the *Catechism*. Thankfully this is less true in the treatment of the Holy Spirit found in the final section of Part One. It is to this topic that we now turn.

HOLY SPIRIT

The *Catechism's* writers introduce the Holy Spirit in the context of Christ's resurrection, asserting that in the resurrection ". . . the three divine persons act together as one, and manifest their own proper characteristics" (CCC 648). The explicit treatment of the Holy Spirit in Article 8 of Section Two reminds the readers that believers come to know God through the Holy Spirit (CCC 687), and in turn come to know the Holy Spirit in the Church, "a communion living in the faith of the apostles which she transmits" (CCC 688). The mission of the Holy Spirit is "brought to completion in the Church" (CCC 737), through which Christ pours out the anointing and healing activities of the Holy Spirit (CCC 739). What is stunning about the treatment of the Holy Spirit is its brevity. Compared with the treatment of Jesus Christ (257 paragraphs), the Holy Spirit is treated in brief (86 paragraphs). In Section One of this part, we saw that the topic of "faith" received brief treatment, and what little was provided for us functioned as a bridge to the section that followed it. In much the same way that faith paved the way to the Creed, the Holy Spirit paves the way to the *Catechism's* discussion of the Church, a discussion that is much longer (198 paragraphs) than the discussion of Holy Spirit. The Church is described as an outgrowth of the activity of the Holy Spirit in salvation history.

The action of the Holy Spirit is essential to the formation of the Church, as outlined in the paragraph entitled "The Spirit and the Church in the Last Days."[20] In this section, the writers portray the close connection between the love of God and the Spirit, noting that the first effect of God's gift of love is the forgiveness of sin and the restoration of divine likeness lost through sin (CCC 734). Second, the Spirit imbues us with the life of the Trinity, by which power we can bear fruit in the mission of Christ (CCC 735-736). However, "the mission of Christ and the Holy Spirit is brought to completion in the Church" (CCC 737). Let us turn to an examination of the Church as found in the catechism.

CHURCH IN COUNCIL AND CATECHISM: SOURCES AND DIRECTIONS

The catechism presents the Church in four basic parts: (a) the Church in God's plan, (b) the Church as people of God, Body of Christ, temple of the Holy Spirit; (c) the marks or notes of the Church (as one, holy, catholic and apostolic); and (d) Christ's faithful: hierarchy, laity, and the consecrated life. The selection of these four parts as the designated topics makes sense to the reader when one considers the final version of *Lumen Gentium*, the dogmatic constitution on the Church from Vatican II.

In its preparation, *Lumen Gentium* underwent several changes in its scope and its theology. The topics covered in the *Catechism* parallel the topics and sequence found in the final version of *Lumen Gentium*. The conciliar document actually covered the following topics in this sequence: the mystery of the Church, the people of God, the hierarchical structure of the Church, with special concern for the episcopate; the laity; the call of the whole Church to holiness; religious life; the pilgrim Church and its relationship to the heavenly Church; the role of Mary, Mother of God in the Church's life.

Interestingly, the Second Vatican Council also produced a document on the Church in the modern world; entitled *Gaudium et Spes* (GS), meaning "Joy and Hope," this document received the special designation of a pastoral constitution. *Gaudium et Spes* complemented the theological treatment of the Church found in the dogmatic constitution, *Lumen Gentium*, and offered an understanding of the Church's relationship to society, culture, and the world in general. Curiously, the pastoral constitution does not receive much attention in the discussion of the Church, while the dogmatic constitution certainly functions as the skeleton for the theology that the catechism enfleshes.

The reader will need to approach this section of the *Catechism* with the knowledge that the writers develop a theology of the Church "from above'' and heavily stress the institutional and universal character of the Church, rather than the communal character of the various churches that are part of the universal Church. This particular point of view is evident throughout the section on the Church. For the sake of brevity, we will examine the four basic themes that shape the description of the Church. Following that examination, we will raise the question "Who ministers in the Church?" Let us turn first to the four main themes treated in this section on the Church found in the *Catechism*.

FOUR THEMES ON THE CHURCH

In reviewing the four themes, the reader will note that the style of writing approximates the catechetical and liturgical language that we found in the presentation of Christology from above. This style does not embrace the findings of historical scholarship about the writings of the Hebrew or Christian testaments, and betrays a lamentable lack of attention to the principles for historical critical thinking that Section One applauded. Since the *Catechism* is intended for an educated audience of catechetical leaders, the lack of attention to various findings from Catholic biblical and historical scholarship is curious. Some examples may serve to illustrate.

The section entitled "The Church in God's Plan" helps the reader to review the ways in which the Church is brought about by its foreshadowing in creation, in the old covenant, and in the ministry of Jesus.[21] The Church is foreshadowed in creation in the sense that from the dawn of time God created humans for communion with divine life; quoting Clement of Alexandria, the writers of the *Catechism* sum up this line of thinking: "Just as God's will is creation and is called 'the world,' so his intention is the salvation . . . and it is called the Church" (CCC 760). But the foreshadowing continues in the development of the old covenant; according to the *Catechism*, the remote preparation for the Church can be found in the narrative of Abram's call and God's promise of descendants. Prophets in Israel who recognized the breach of the covenant foretold the establishment of a new covenant (CCC 761-762).

According to the *Catechism*, Jesus' ministry foreshadowed the leadership structure of the Church even in its current structure through the selection of the Twelve Apostles: "The Lord Jesus endowed his community with a structure that will remain until the kingdom is fully achieved. Before all else there is the choice of the Twelve with Peter as their head'' (CCC 765). The writers of the *Catechism* seem to have ignored the findings of biblical scholars in the last three decades as they have unearthed the multiple expressions of Church life in the various churches throughout the ancient world. Moreover, these scholars have come to the knowledge that there were a variety of leadership models present in these churches.

A second theme for the *Catechism* is the truth that the Church is a mystery. Echoing the theology of *Lumen Gentium,* the *Catechism* describes the Church as both a visible and a spiritual reality (CCC 771).[22] It is both a visible and spiritual reality in much the same way as a sacrament is understood; in fact, the writers note that the Eastern churches refer to sacraments as *mysteries.* This section does not include a development of the idea of sacrament, a theme that is proper to Part Two. However, the section relies heavily on the eighth article of *Lumen Gentium,* and thus it treats the Church in both its external and internal dimensions; it is described as both a visible assembly and a spiritual community. Further, this section seeks to highlight the Church's vocation to reflect the connection between the union of God and humanity, reaching its perfect expression in Jesus Christ, and the unity among all human beings (CCC 775).

A third theme on the Church concerns a threefold description through the use of three familiar images: The Church as people of God, Body of Christ, and temple of the Holy Spirit. In the case of the first image, the reader harkens back to the connection (already established) between the Holy Spirit and the Church, since the people are more than a sociological group; they are formed by the Spirit in individual and communal ways (CCC 781-782). Here the *Catechism* relies on the ideas set forth in *Lumen Gentium* (LG 9), in order to assert that the Spirit is the impetus for the conscious plan to form the people of God. For the image of Christ's body (CCC 787-796), the writers again draw heavily upon *Lumen Gentium* (LG 7), which in turn relies on passages from the epistles in order to assert that Christ is the head of the body. Curiously the review of the epistles does not lead the writers to the discussion found in 1 Corinthians about the variety and diversity of gifts, but leads instead to the reassertion of the Church as the obedient bride of Christ (CCC 796). The call to obedience to the institutional life of the Church is sounded again through the use of the third and final image, the temple of the Holy Spirit. Treatment of that image ends with these words regarding the charisms or gifts of the Holy Spirit:

It is in this sense that discernment of charisms is always necessary. No charism is exempt from being referred and submitted to the Church's shepherds. "Their office [is] not indeed to extinguish the Spirit, but to test all things and hold fast to what is good," so that all the diverse and complementary charisms work together "for the common good" (CCC 801).

From the review of these four themes, we can see that the writers emphasize those aspects of the universal Church that make it a visible reality in our world, and the internal authority that forms the Church as an institution. This is further corroborated by considering the question "Who ministers in the Church?," according to this *Catechism*.

MINISTRY IN THE CHURCH

The writers of the *Catechism* confine the use of the term "ministry" to the ordained only; there is no use of that term in relation to the work of lay persons. The description of the ministry occurs in the context of the hierarchical structure of the Church. This description begins with the review of *Lumen Gentium* (LG 18), which states that Christ instituted a variety of ministries directed toward the good of the whole people of God.[23] However, the next article in the *Catechism* states that "the ministry of the Church is conferred by a special sacrament" (CCC 875). Conversely, lay persons fulfill their mission by evangelization "in the ordinary circumstances of the world" (CCC 905),[24] and through family life and effective parenting (CCC 901-902). Quoting the *Code of Canon Law*, the *Catechism* indicates that where the Church's needs require it and *ministers* are not available, lay people may supply certain of their functions (CCC 903).[25] So we can see that the terms "minister" and "ministry" do not refer to those in the ministry of catechetical leadership who daily refer to themselves as such and who are the likely readers of the *Catechism*.

To summarize: The writers of the *Catechism* rely on a selective use of the documents from Vatican II in order to present images of the Church as the fruit of the ministry of Jesus and the work of the Holy Spirit. In so doing, they employ a language that is more reflective than analytical, and thus this section may not provide the doctrinal information that its readers seek. The writers tend to develop the notion of the Church as an institution with strong authorities who are responsible for the life of the Church. This approach of ecclesiology "from above'' is not complemented by discussions of the variety and diversity of practices in the local churches of the New Testament era, of the variety and diversity of gifts of the Spirit in the churches, or of the variety and diversity of the ministries present in those local churches and retrieved in "ministry" language and practice in the three decades since the Second Vatican Council.

CATECHISM: END OR BEGINNING?

In this chapter we have examined salient features of Part One. From Section One of this part, we have recognized the organizing dynamic for revelation to be the interplay between God's gracious invitation and the human response to this invitation. The mode through which we come to know God is our own history, particularly when that history is viewed through the lens of faith as a history of salvation.

These claims about revelation are relatively recent ones in the mainline thinking of Catholic theologians and catechetical leaders. The claims rest on newly acquired knowledge about the sources of revelation: Scripture and tradition. This newly acquired knowledge results from the use of newly applied methods of research into the meaning of biblical texts and the intention of early Christian writers.

From Section Two of Part One, we have excised those items treated in the Apostles' Creed that the *Catechism* covers extensively; they are Jesus Christ, the centerpiece of Christian revelation, and the Church, the context in which our Christian response in faith is celebrated, supported, and challenged.

The *Catechism* is intended primarily for the bishops as an instrument for use in teaching; it is also addressed to editors, priests, catechists, and all others responsible for catechesis (CCC 12). The *Catechism* is intended to serve these catechetical leaders "as a point of reference for the catechisms *or compendia* to be composed in the various countries."[26] A critical reading of Part One raises some issues concerning the use of the text in the catechetical enterprise.

In view of the intended audience for the *Catechism*, who will actually make use of Part One? How do these catechetical leaders who are not bishops or priests understand their role and membership in the Church? Do the lay leaders who are responsible for catechesis think of themselves as ministers of the Word? How will they read and receive the description of ministry in the Church as found in Part One?

Second, how do the lay catechetical leaders who will refer to Part One understand their mission in relationship to the mission of Jesus? To the mission of ordained ministers today?

Third, how do the catechetical leaders understand Jesus Christ as a human being as well as the second Person of the Trinity? In articulating their understanding of Jesus Christ, how will they reconcile the insights from their professional education with the treatment of Jesus Christ found in Part One?

Related to this is a fourth concern. How do the catechetical leaders who will use this part understand the relationship among Jesus' ministry, the New Testament faith of Jesus' followers, and the nature and function of the Church today? Is that understanding compatible with the ecclesiology contained in Part One?

Finally, what do catechetical leaders hope for their Church? Will the *Catechism* aid them in realizing those hopes? How?

In conclusion, we might do well to understand that the *Catechism of the Catholic Church* is not the end of the search to provide catechesis. It is a beginning. It is a source to which leaders may turn first, but they may not stop there. It should be used in the context of Vatican II, which has informed Catholic theological and catechetical thought in the twentieth century, a council whose effects we have only begun to experience and whose vision provides the backdrop for attending to the material of the *Catechism*. That task has only begun.

For Further Reading

On the topic of revelation, the most celebrated contemporary work is Avery Dulles, *Models of Revelation* (Garden City, N.Y.: Doubleday, 1983). In that work, Dulles sets out the notion of models and explains why models are helpful to theology and especially to crafting various ways to envision revelation. The "propositional" model and the model of "revelation as history" provide foundation for the discussion of Section One of Part One.

On the issue of the knowability of God in and through revelation, see Dermot A. Lane, *The Experience of God: An Invitation to Do Theology* (New York: Paulist, 1981). This work, when read alongside Dulles' models, provides excellent background to the arguments set forth in the opening section of Part One in the *Catechism*. Each of these texts assumes the understanding of revelation as divine invitation as set forth in Vatican II and in the catechism.

For adult groups who seek specific foundations to the study of the Creed in accessible reading for non-specialists, the following may be helpful: Kathleen Fisher and Thomas Hart, *Christian Foundations* (New York: Paulist, 1983); Mariann H. Micks, *Loving the Questions: An Exploration of the Nicene Creed* (Valley Forge, Penn.: Trinity Press International, 1993); Neil Ormerod, *Introducing Contemporary Theologies: The What and the Who of Theology Today* (Newtown, Australia: E.J. Dwyer, 1990). These works lend the interested student of theology a prism through which to regard contemporary Catholic theology in a general sense, with frequent reference to the applicability and relevance of the Creed to contemporary Church life. In treating the Creed, each of them guides the reader through the theology of revelation exhibited in *Dei Verbum*.

The area of the *Catechism* for which supplementary reading would be most enlightening is Section Two of Part One, which deals with Christology. The following provide excellent summaries of contemporary findings in biblical scholarship about Jesus and in the resultant Christologies that capture the attention of contemporary theologians.

Michael L. Cook, *Responses to 101 Questions About Jesus* (New York: Paulist, 1993) provides a summation of biblical scholarship on Jesus, and would enrich adult education group discussions and programs. Joseph A. Fitzmyer, *A Christological Catechism: New Testament Answers* (Ramsey, N.J.: Paulist Press, 1982) also provides summation in a similar style. Fitzmyer represents the kind of Catholic biblical scholarship done since the Second Vatican council in a way that is clear in style yet challenging in scope to novice readers.

Brennan Hill, *Jesus the Christ: Contemporary Perspectives* (Mystic, Conn.: Twenty-Third Publications, 1991) offers a Christology that respects the historical critical findings, the scriptural data, and early Christological councils. Hill presents the contemporary Christological questions about Jesus in a method that is sensitive to the concerns of liberation and feminist theologies. Hill offers the same challenge to non-historically minded readers as does Albert Nolan in *Jesus Before Christianity* (Maryknoll, N.Y.: Orbis Books, 1992 revision). The cultural and social setting of Jesus of Nazareth and the first disciples is presented effectively in Gerard S. Sloyan, *Jesus In Focus: A Life in its Setting* (Mystic, Conn.: Twenty-Third Publications, 1983). Elizabeth A. Johnson, *Consider Jesus: Waves of Renewal in Christology* (New York:

Crossroad, 1990) stands out as a collection of essays on the contemporary state of Christology. The author is able to present both the findings of biblical scholarship on the historical Jesus and those insights from systematic theology that complement biblical research. Johnson adopts a Christology from Karl Rahner that is both readable and compelling to the beginning student of Christology.

Catechetical leaders who seek an introduction for learners who are completely unfamiliar with biblical analysis will benefit from reviewing James P. McIlhone, *The Word Made Clear: A Guide to the Bible for Contemporary Catholic Readers* (Chicago, Ill.: Thomas More Press, 1992). Serious readers who want to pursue the current state of scholarship on the historical Jesus will be challenged and rewarded by reading John P. Meier, *A Marginal Jew: Rethinking the Historical Jesus* (New York: Doubleday, 1991). Meier reviews the "roots of the problem and the person" in this work. The author promises that this book is only the first in a trilogy that can be accrued to a careful reading of the New Testament research and an understanding of Christology from below as well as from above.

On the topic of the Church, a contemporary ecclesiology is introduced to novice theologians in Dennis M. Doyle, *The Church Emerging from Vatican II* (Mystic, Conn.: Twenty-Third Publications, 1992). Doyle uses *Lumen Gentium* as the framework for introducing ecclesiology from the council and several important current questions in ecclesiology. Since the council, much has been written on the theme of ministry and its relationship to the internal identity and respective roles of Church members, lay and ordained. Two foundational works are Edward Schillebeeckx, *Ministry: Leadership in the Community of Jesus Christ* (New York: Crossroad, 1981), and Thomas Franklin O'Meara, *Theology of Ministry* (New York: Paulist, 1983). Each of these offers historical and systematic presentations that illumine the pastoral situations which many Catholics face within parish life. Appropriate reading for the newcomer to this topic includes Richard McBrien, *Ministry: A Theological, Pastoral Handbook* (San Francisco: Harper and Row, 1987) and William J. Bausch, *Ministry: Traditions, Tensions, Transitions* (Mystic, Conn.: Twenty-Third Publications, 1982).

Notes for Chapter 4

1. This affirmation is found in the document on the liturgy, entitled *Sacrosanctum Concilium,* and in the *Rite of Christian Initiation of Adults,* which was restored in the Catholic Church after Vatican Council II. It is the basis for the presentation of revelation found in the *General Catechetical Directory* and in *Sharing the Light of Faith, the National Catechetical Directory for Catholics in the United States.*

2. This is not to suggest that this essay can offer an exhaustive treatment of these sources from Vatican II. Rather we will turn to a few representative documents from the council. These sources merely signal the larger trend found in a sustained reading and analysis of the documents themselves.

3. For example, the treatment of revelation in significant documents about catechesis reflects the theology of revelation articulated at Vatican II. Two important documents that display this are the *General Catechetical Directory* and *Sharing the Light of Faith, the National Catechetical Directory for Catholics in the United States.*

4. The status of a dogmatic constitution is a signal about the importance given by the council fathers to this topic. Not all the council documents were accorded this status.

5. The catechism develops this idea in paragraph 62.

6. This item has received much attention since the council. *Dei Verbum* 4 states that ''. . . no new public revelation is to be expected before the glorious manifestation of our Lord, Jesus Christ.'' The catechism quotes this in the text of paragraph 66.

7. No document is quoted more or more concurrently; note that there are entire narratives in which the footnotes to the text are references to successive articles in *Dei Verbum.* This pattern is virtually unbroken in chapter two of Book 1, concerning ''God's Initiative'' (CCC 50-133).

8. *Dei Verbum* 2 also develops this idea.

9. See *Dei Verbum* 9.

10. For a fuller treatment of this topic, see Avery Dulles, *Models of Revelation* and Dermot Lane, *The Experience of God: An Invitation to Do Theology,* treated in the bibliographical essay at the conclusion of this chapter.

11. Avery Dulles, *Models of Revelation,* (Garden City, N.Y.: Doubleday, 1983).

12. This treatment has its limitations because it tends toward the supercessionism that denigrates the integrity of the revelation in Judaism. For a critique of this thinking found in the catechism see Leon Klenicki, ''Catechism of the Catholic Church: A Concerned Jewish Reading,'' *Professional Approaches for Christian Educators (PACE)* 23 (April 1994). Attempting to meet that concern, the writers of the *Catechism* try to reject the Marcionite tendencies in Christianity in that same article. Marcion, who died in the mid-second century, rejected the validity of the Hebrew testament revelation in favor of the Christian revelation, and was condemned as a heretic for his lack of attention to the integrity of the entire bible as the Christians regarded it.

13. Note that CCC 126 nearly replicates the words of *Dei Verbum,* 19.

14. Note that *Dei Verbum* presents this same material by reference to the ''situation of the *churches.''* The catechism reads: ''. . . in terms of the *Church's* current situation.'' This distinction is a curious one, as the Vatican Council document seems to respect that the early Church was comprised of many churches with various interpretations based in diverse situations, while the catechism refers only to the universal Church. In the context of this discussion about the composition of the Gospels, it seems appropriate to refer to the *churches,* since scholarship about this period in Christian history would concur that there were a variety of interpretations and situations. See for example the work of Michael Cook and John Meier in the bibliographical essay which appears at the conclusion of this chapter.

15. Gnostic Docetism, Nestorianism, and Monophysitism are mentioned and briefly defined in the catechism (465, 466, and 467 respectively). Monothelitism — the belief that Jesus Christ possessed only one will and therefore was not fully human — is not expressly mentioned, but the affirmation of the Council of Constantinople III in 681, over against the Monothelite claim, is taken up in paragraph 475.

16. *Guidelines and Suggestions for Implementing the Conciliar Declaration "Nostra Aetate,"* 4.

17. Some contemporary examples of contextual theology are liberation theology, feminist theology, and black theology. This is not to say that other theological projects are done without a context. Indeed, these contextual theologies have helped theologians recognize the assumptions and even biases that are brought to the task of theology or the task of analyzing sacred texts. The specific matrix that informs contextual theologies is that of oppression and the liberating power of the gospel. On the issue of contextual theologies, see Rosemary Radford Ruether, ed., *To Change the World: Christology and Cultural Criticism,* (New York: Crossroad, 1981).

18. For a variety of essays on the topic, see W. Willis, ed., *The Kingdom of God in Twentieth Century Interpretation,* (Peabody, Mass.: Hendrickson Publishers, 1987).

19. In this section of the *Catechism*, the discussion of the need to adjust catechesis to the age and culture and particular level of faith in the catechized comes to us from both the *Catechism of the Council of Trent* ("Roman Catechism") (in the preface) and *Catechesi Tradendae,* 20–22.

20. CCC 731-741 establishes this bridge between the respective sections on the Holy Spirit and the Church.

21. CCC 760-765 treat each of these in turn.

22. CCC 771 refers directly to *Lumen Gentium,* 8.

23. CCC 874 quotes *Lumen Gentium,* 18.

24. This article refers directly to *Lumen Gentium,* 35.

25. This article refers to the *Code of Canon Law,* can. 230.

26. CCC 11, quoting the *Final Report* of the Synod of Bishops, 1985.

CHAPTER 5

The Celebration of the Christian Mystery

Jane E. Regan

In the Creed, the Church professes its core beliefs; in the liturgy the Church celebrates that which it professes. At the heart of the Creed is the affirmation of the mystery of the Trinity and of God's saving action in all of creation. At the heart of the liturgical life of the Church is the celebration of the paschal mystery and Christ's redemptive action. What is professed in the Creed is celebrated in the Church's liturgy.

Part Two, "The Celebration of the Christian Mystery," sets out for the reader the richness and depth of the Church's liturgical life and its expression in the celebration of the sacraments. As with the other parts of the *Catechism*, Part Two is divided into two sections. Section One, "The Sacramental Economy," begins with an examination of our understanding of liturgy, seeing it in its broadest sense as our response to, and participation in, God's redemptive work. Since the Eucharist and the other sacraments are at the heart of the Church's liturgical life (CCC 1113), the first section of Part Two then continues by setting out the concept of sacrament as it has developed within our theological tradition. Section One then concludes with a discussion of the elements of sacramental celebrations that are common to all of the sacraments. Section Two, "The Seven Sacraments of the Church," examines each of the sacraments individually.

This chapter begins with an exploration of the notion of liturgy that configures our approach to sacraments. Since our concept of liturgy is reflective of the Vatican II document on liturgy, some time is spent situating this discussion within the *Constitution on the Sacred Liturgy*. Returning to the *Catechism*, the interplay between our understanding of liturgy and our approach to the seven sacraments is explored. The final section of this chapter attempts to draw the connection between the core principles set out in Section One, "The Sacramental Economy," and the more specific discussion of each of the sacraments examined in Section Two, "The Seven Sacraments."

SACRAMENT AS LITURGY

Before one enters into the discussion of a particular sacrament, before one launches into an exploration of the specific rituals, it is essential that the foundational framework for discussing sacraments in general be set out. The tendency to focus on an individual sacrament makes it easy to miss the broader context for the possibility of the existence of sacraments in the first place. What is the understanding of the relationship between God and human beings that makes possible the reality of the sacramental life of the Church? Part Two, "Celebration of the Christian Mystery," chooses to examine the framework for the discussion of sacraments under the general rubric of liturgy.

As set out in Section One of Part Two, liturgy is understood not primarily in terms of celebrations of specific acts of prayer and worship but in the broader terms of human participation in God's work of redemption.

> In Christian tradition [liturgy] means the participation of the People of God in "the work of God." Through the liturgy Christ, our redeemer and high priest, continues the work of our redemption in, with, and through his Church (CCC 1069).

In liturgy the faith community gathers to remember God's saving work particularly in Jesus Christ, to celebrate God's action within the life of the community, and to express our ongoing confidence in God's loving presence into the future.

In the previous chapter's exploration of Part One, "The Profession of Faith," it was made clear that the discussion of the Creed is situated in the broader context of the relationship between revelation and faith. Reflective of the discussion that marked Vatican II, and at the heart of our understanding of revelation, is the invitation-response dynamic. Revelation consists of God's self-communication and continuing invitation to human beings to be in relationship with God. Faith is the human response to this divine invitation. The very same dynamic is at the heart of liturgy and of the sacramental life of the Church.

Liturgy here is understood as a dialogue that emanates from God. It is God's proactive presence of blessing and redemption that is the originating source of liturgy. From the dawn of creation to the fulfillment of history at the end time, God's work of salvation is given expression. Our response to the mystery of God's love is worship, praise, and surrender (cf. CCC 1077-1083).

The reality of God's presence has been expressed clearly and definitively in the saving work of Jesus Christ. Thus, at the heart of all liturgical action, and expressed most clearly in the sacraments, is the celebration of the paschal mystery.

> In the liturgy of the Church, it is primarily his own Paschal mystery that Christ signifies and makes present. During his earthly life Jesus announced his Paschal mystery by his teaching and anticipated it by his actions. When his Hour comes, he lives out the unique event of history which does not pass away: Jesus dies, is buried, rises from the dead and is seated at the right hand of the Father "once for all" (CCC 1085).

Through liturgy, the community of faith enters into the one saving mystery of life, death, and resurrection. In that one mystery we are connected with one another and become participants in that saving action.

The dialogue that is at the heart of all liturgy is initiated by God and rooted in the paschal mystery of Christ. But the human side of that dialogue is made possible by the presence of the Holy Spirit. It is through the Holy Spirit that the assembly is united and connected to the one mystery of Christ (CCC 1104). Liturgy is essentially Trinitarian. It is the Trinity that serves as source, goal, and animator for the gathering of believers.

In summary, the introductory pages of Part Two present an understanding of liturgy that serves as the framework for the discussion of the sacramental life of the Church and of the individual sacraments. At the core of liturgy is the God-initiated dialogue between God and human beings: God's saving presence in word and action begins the dialogue; prayer and worship is our response. This dialogue is rooted in, and gives expression to, the paschal mystery: the saving death and resurrection of Jesus Christ. Through the working of the Holy Spirit, that mystery is present at each liturgical event, and the gathered community of believers participate in that saving work.

In its exploration of liturgy, the *Catechism of the Catholic Church* relies heavily on the document from the Second Vatican Council that served as the point of reference for the liturgical renewal as it came to expression over the past thirty years: the *Constitution on the Sacred Liturgy* (*Sacrosanctum Concilium* [SC]) Since Section One of Part Two draws so heavily from this document, our reading of Part Two can be enhanced by an examination of its focus and significance.

"THE CONSTITUTION ON THE SACRED LITURGY"

The *Constitution on the Sacred Liturgy* begins by situating the discussion of the reform of the liturgy within the context of the general purpose of the council itself. Since this was the first of the documents promulgated (December 4, 1963), the overall aims of the council were briefly stated in its opening paragraph:

> . . . to impart an ever-increasing vigor to the Christian life of the faithful; to adapt more closely to the needs of our age those institutions which are subject to change; to foster whatever can promote union among all who believe in Christ; to strengthen whatever can help to call all mankind into the Church's fold. (SC 1)[1]

In the years following the document's publication, it has become clear that the reform and renewal of the liturgy both facilitate the goals of the council and reflect the expression of those goals in various aspects of the Church's life.

As with a number of other documents discussed and promulgated in the context of Vatican II, the document on the liturgy had been drafted by a preparatory commission in the year before the council. However, unlike some of the other draft documents, the one on the liturgy was only slightly changed in light of conciliar discussions. While the diligent work of the Preparatory Liturgical Commission certainly gets some acknowledgment, the relative unanimity among the bishops concerning liturgical reform is a direct outcome of the powerful influence of the liturgical movement during the decades leading up to Vatican II.

Since no council takes place in a vacuum, one could argue that all the topics discussed at Vatican II had their origin and impetus in the life of the Church. However, there were few topics that had received the international attention that had been given to the liturgy in the decades leading up to this council. And there were few dimensions of Church life more "ripe" for reform. It is beyond the scope of this chapter to detail the evolution of the modern liturgical movement.[2] One would have to make reference to a range of influences in the early nineteenth century and pay particular attention to the work of Benedictine Dom Prosper Guéranger, as he brought to the fore the problems inherent to liturgy in nineteenth-century France and the central role the liturgy could play in the life of the Church. The interplay of the liturgical movement with the developments in biblical scholarship and the renewal of catechesis contributed to the richness of the theological and pastoral foundations that guided liturgical renewal during the early twentieth century.[3]

Even as renewal was taking place, the liturgy was also undergoing reform, that is, authoritative emendations and improvements in the liturgical rites themselves. Pope Pius X in the early decades of the twentieth century restored the use of Gregorian chant and, more significantly for the people, encouraged frequent, even daily, Communion, and Communion for children at the age of reason. Under Pius X the liturgical calendar was cleared a bit in order to give precedence to the Sunday celebration and to the observance of Lent. Pope Pius XII picked up the task of reform and established a pontifical commission responsible for the restoration of the liturgy. In the 1950s the commission revised the rite of the Easter Vigil and then all of the Holy Week services. It worked to simplify the rubrics and define the parameters of liturgical participation by the people. Attention was also given to liturgical disciplines, such as the shortening of the eucharistic fast and the introduction of bilingual rituals (Latin and the vernacular).

It was the decades-long experience of the complementarity between renewal and reform that prepared the way for the almost unanimous acceptance of the schema of the *Constitution on the Sacred Liturgy* and the subsequent approval of the document itself during the second session of Vatican II. In many ways, this document crystallized the principles that had guided the reform during the first half of the century and provided the impetus for continuing the reform and renewal.

The content of the *Constitution on the Sacred Liturgy* reflects this dynamic relationship between reform and the principles that direct the reform. While there are significant sections that set out the directives for specific liturgical changes, there are also paragraphs that attend to doctrinal foundations and the principles of reform.[4] As the new rites for liturgical celebrations were introduced in the years following the council, the practical sections of the document were addressed and even superseded. The more theoretical elements of the constitution, however, have continued to shape the direction of liturgical theology over the past thirty years. It is to these sections of the council document that the *Catechism of the Catholic Church* makes reference.

A review of the footnotes of Section One of Part Two makes clear its dependence on the *Constitution on the Sacred Liturgy:* all but a handful of the almost thirty pages include references to the Constitution. In many places the discussion in the *Catechism* follows the presentation in the conciliar document paragraph by paragraph. Section One of Part Two draws particularly on the introduction and the first two sections of chapter I of the Constitution, where the nature of the liturgy and its importance to the life of the Church are explored. The fundamental conception of liturgy that shapes the discussion in the *Catechism* is drawn from these pages in the Constitution and serves as foundation to the more specific discussion of the sacraments. It is to this discussion that we now turn.

THE CHURCH'S SACRAMENTS

What are the implications of the renewed understanding of liturgy reflected in the *Constitution on the Sacred Liturgy* and then in the *Catechism of the Catholic Church* for how we are to understand the Church's seven sacraments? What is the impact on our sacramental theology and practice to say that liturgy — the broad category within which the specific sacraments gain meaning — is perceived as a remembrance and a celebration of God's continuing redemptive presence? In what ways are our theology and practice affected when we affirm that the sacraments return us to the reality of the paschal mystery and provide us with a way of participating in that saving event? What is the significance of attesting to the fundamentally Trinitarian nature of the sacraments and recognizing the Holy Spirit's role in making present the mystery of God's love at each liturgical event? The *Catechism* attempts to give response to these questions in Article 2 of the first chapter of Part Two, "The Paschal Mystery in the Church's Sacraments."

The complexity of the reality of sacraments is made clear in this article, as the discussion explores five distinct yet related dimensions to our understanding of sacraments (1114-1130). The sacraments are first, "sacraments of Christ": they point to the words and actions of Jesus that anticipated the reality of the paschal mystery. Second, we speak of the sacraments as "sacraments of the Church": they flow from the Church's desire to give expression to the mystery mediated by Christ and they communicate and disclose the essence of the Church itself. The Church here is seen as a priestly community empowered and built up by the celebration of the sacraments. From another perspective the sacraments are seen as "sacraments of faith": they both presuppose faith and nourish and strengthen it. Additionally, the Church confesses what it believes in the celebration of the sacraments; as the Church, we believe as we pray (*lex orandi, lex credendi*). Fourth, the sacraments are "sacraments of salvation": it is Christ who is at work in each sacramental event; it is the power of the Spirit that transforms and effects salvation. And, finally, the sacraments are "sacraments of eternal life": in each celebration of the sacraments, the Church anticipates the end time when Christ will come again and all human hope will be fulfilled.

These five categories for grasping the nature of the sacraments are helpful and invite us to explore the reality of sacraments further. We can enhance and augment the understanding set out in the *Catechism* by situating its discussion within the broader conversation of the shifts that have taken place within sacramental theology in the context of the promulgation of the *Constitution on the Sacred Liturgy*. There fundamental shifts in the understanding of sacraments can serve as foundations to the doctrinal description given in Article 2.[5] The shifts spoken of here do not involve the rejection of one perspective in favor of another, but the balancing of two perspectives that have not always been kept in tandem.

1. A SHIFT FROM SEEING SACRAMENTS AS MEANS by which God breaks into the secular world to seeing sacraments as effective symbols of God's always present action in a world graced by the divine presence.

As profound symbols,[6] the sacraments stand as "doors to the sacred": they point to and mark God's presence in human history, in the life of the Church and in a particular community of faith. They celebrate all that God is doing in our lives. In this context, the notion of a two-tiered world consisting of a profane existence that is sometimes penetrated by the action of God is set aside in favor of the unified reality of God's always present offer of divine love.

God's presence is always part of human life, and that presence is marked from time to time with the celebration of sacraments. A birthday celebration makes sense when it points to or marks our gratefulness for the gift of life and for the presence of the particular person whose birthday we celebrate; the birthday celebration is the opportunity to bring into focus the deep reality of love and care that shape our day-to-day lives. In a similar way, the sacraments make most sense when they highlight for us the essential elements of our most authentic relationships with God, with ourselves, and with one another. At core, the key elements of authentic relations have been exemplified for us in the life and teaching of Jesus; they are to be characterized by the experience of community, the reality of forgiveness, the importance of commitment, the experience of welcoming new members, and so on. It is the relationships the sacraments point to that provide the deep meaning of the sacramental event. We can speak of the sacraments here as moments of intensification in which our awareness of God's presence is intentionally heightened.

In the sacraments we are invited not only to be aware of God's presence but to respond to that presence as well. In the sacramental event we respond first with praise and worship. But this heightened awareness also has an effect on who we understand ourselves to be and how we live our lives. This moves us to the second major shift.

2. A SHIFT FROM SEEING THE SAVING EFFECT OF SACRAMENTS as solely a future reality to recognizing their effect in the present.

There is a future element to the salvific nature of sacraments: they connect us with God's grace in our lives and we anticipate the fulfillment of that at the end time. But there is also a present dimension — our salvation is not simply in the "here after"; it is also here and now. Sacraments are effective symbols because they point to the reality of a world marked by God's presence *and* they contribute to bringing that world to fulfillment.

Through the sacramental event our awareness of God's grace in our lives is deepened, and our response is prayer, praise, and — ultimately — action. Through the sacraments we are challenged and empowered by the Spirit to live lives reflective of God's presence; we are empowered to reflect in our relationships with self and others those same characteristics that typified Jesus's relationships. In this sense, we are called to transform our lives in order to be sacraments to one another and to the world: to be effective symbols of God's presence.

While this transformation or conversion of our lives to configure with the values and perspectives inherent in the sacraments takes place on an individual basis; it always happens within the context of the Christian community. The Church is the gathering of people dedicated to bringing to fullness the reality of God's presence in the present. It is here, then, that we can speak about the Church as sacrament: the Church's task is to give evidence of the presence of God by giving expression to God's presence in the world today. In its internal relationships and in its relationship with the world, the Church's words and actions are to be marked by gospel values.[7]

3. A SHIFT FROM SEEING SACRAMENTS as something done to individuals to seeing them as identity-expressing actions of a community. With the reform of the rites following Vatican II, this shift has probably been one of the most evident. Setting the celebration of baptism, confirmation, and marriage within the context of the eucharistic liturgy, establishing rituals for the communal celebration of the sacrament of reconciliation, situating the anointing of the sick within the broader context of pastoral care expressed by various members of the community: each of these reforms was designed to contribute to the renewal of the sacraments as community celebrations.

As community celebrations, the sacraments are identity forming. Just as a family's values and identity are disclosed and strengthened by the times and settings of family gatherings, so too is the identity of the Christian community. We know who we are and what we are called to be as a community through these sacramental events.

These shifts in our understanding of sacraments lead to an emphasis that sees the sacraments as community events that call individuals and communities to transform their lives and to expand their awareness of God's redemptive presence. Like all theological developments, these shifts in our sense of sacraments do not take place in a vacuum. The evident interplay between our understanding of sacraments and our sense of the nature of the Church, the person of Jesus, the realities of human nature, and the relationship between God and human beings makes clear that the shifts discussed here have wide implication. To understand their significance, let us look more closely at the fundamental theological understanding that sustains them.

GRACE: THE GIFT OF GOD'S LOVE

As was stated earlier, to speak of the sacraments as ways of affirming and celebrating God's presence is incompatible with the separation of human existence into two spheres: sacred and profane. All human activity is brought together in the reality shaped by the presence of

God. The theological concept for this reality is "grace." Behind the change in emphasis in our understanding of sacraments, and sustaining it, is a shift in our conception of grace.

The relegation of the human enterprise to a secular or profane world sees one's relationship with God as an addition to human life, as outside day-to-day existence. Within this concept of human life, one's relationship with God is established and furthered by the grace that God gives in discrete quantities from some place outside of us. Within this framework, the sacraments primarily serve not to mark and celebrate God's presence but somehow to influence God to give us some grace.

The alternate notion of grace that is at the heart of our renewed sense of sacraments sees grace not as an item but as the integral gift of God's life and love. From this perspective, grace is always, in every moment of human life, being offered; the very offer of grace is essential to the possibility of being human. To be human is to be open to this offer of grace, to be open to the free gift of God's life.

The person who writes most clearly about this notion of grace is Karl Rahner, who speaks in terms of a "world of grace," a world defined by the reality of God's free offer of grace. Rahner makes clear that within his theological framework grace is not a quantifiable reality;

> Instead, it is the comprehensive radical opening up of the person's total consciousness in the direction of the immediacy of God, an opening up that is brought about by God's own self-communication.[8]

Within this offer of grace is the invitation to self-transcendence, a self-transcendence that is constitutive to being human. And part of the offer includes the freedom to say no; there is a difference between God's always and everywhere offer of grace and human acceptance.

Relevant to this discussion is another component of Rahner's understanding of grace: grace can be experienced. We do experience moments of self-transcendence. In his essay "Reflections of the Experience of Grace," Rahner invites us to reflect on those experiences that have at their foundation the reality of grace.

> Have we ever kept quiet, even though we wanted to defend ourselves when we had been unfairly treated? Have we ever forgiven someone even though we got no thanks for it and our silent forgiveness was taken for granted? Have we ever obeyed, not because we had to and because otherwise things would have become unpleasant for us, but simply on account of that mysterious, silent,

incomprehensible being we call God and his will? . . . Have we ever decided on some course of action purely by the innermost judgment of our conscience, deep down where one can no longer tell or explain it to anyone, where one is quite alone and knows that one is taking a decision which no one else can take in one's place and for which one will have to answer for all eternity? . . .[9]

Grace comes to expression in relationships and in the concrete decisions of our lives. Whether it is experienced as essential hope in the face of hopelessness or as radical self-giving with no expectation of return, its articulation is fundamentally interpersonal or social.

Given this understanding of grace, it is clear that the sacraments do not "give grace" if by that is meant the distribution of an item from outside human reality. Sacraments "give grace" because they embody the reality of God's offer of grace; they affirm and celebrate the way in which God's life, i.e., grace, is experienced in human history, in the Church and in a particular faith community. We can speak of the sacraments as giving grace in the sense that they are opportunities for us to respond "Yes!" in a formal way to God's offer of grace. Through the celebration of the sacraments, individuals and communities are opened to the reality of God's world of grace and affirm their desire to participate in that reality.[10]

This understanding of grace leads to viewing the seven sacraments not as discrete actions but as a united expression of the one reality of God's presence. The significance of each sacrament is recognized in its unity with the overall sacramental life of the Church. While it is possible to speak of the meaningfulness of a particular sacrament for the faith community, the fundamental role of the sacraments is seen within the broader intention of giving form to the reality of a world marked by grace. This returns us to the earlier discussion of the sacraments as liturgy. Each sacrament serves as an indicator of the one mystery of God; each sacrament gives expression to the one reality of the paschal mystery celebrated through the liturgy. It is in our continual participation in the paschal mystery that the transformative presence of God is made evident.

In the opening pages of Part Two, the focus of liturgical catechesis is described as the process of initiating people into the mystery of Christ "by proceeding from the visible to the invisible, from the sign to the thing signified, from the 'sacraments' to the 'mysteries' " (CCC 1075). In this discussion of the nature of grace, the mystery to which the sacraments point becomes evident: the depth of the mystery of God's love conveyed in God's free self-communication with us that we call "grace." The complex simplicity of that reality must be the lens through which we examine the elements of liturgical celebration (Chapter Two of Section One) and the particulars of each of the sacraments (Section Two).

CELEBRATING THE SACRAMENTS

The various sacramental rituals have their unity in the mystery to which they point and in the elements they have in common. The second chapter of Section One examines the common elements of sacramental celebrations under these headings: Who celebrates?, How do we celebrate?, When do we celebrate?, Where do we celebrate? Under these headings the dynamics that give shape, form, and power to the Church's rituals are explored.

In the sacramental liturgy it is first and foremost the whole community that celebrates (CCC 1140). Key to liturgical renewal and reform has been the goal of fostering "full conscious and active participation in liturgical celebrations called for by the very nature of the liturgy" (SC 14). This is expressed in the role of the assembly and of the various ministers within the liturgy. The whole assembly acts in the celebration of the sacraments, each one with his or her own function, but all united within the one Spirit (CCC 1144).

At the heart of the ritual itself is the vital interaction among the powerful symbols, words, and actions (1145). Rooted in the Christian story, these core symbols also draw energy from their connection with the story of God's working with the Israelites and from their fundamental connection with the created order. Energy is inherent to such symbol-action-word events as immersing a person in flowing water and pronouncing the words that make clear in whose name we do this.

Each particular liturgical event takes place within a broader context. One element of this is sacred time expressed in the liturgical year and particularly the significance of the Lord's Day (CCC 1163-1171). A second component to that context is sacred space: while at the heart of Christian gathering are the "living stones," the church building itself speaks of God's presence in the world (CCC 1179-1181).

The rituals that form the visible expression of the sacraments are constituted by the people, symbols, actions, and context in which they

occur. The complementary interaction of these different elements con-
tributes to the evocative nature of ritual: more is conveyed in sacramental ritual then can be expressed in words or propositions. Through ritual
we enter into a sacred realm in which conversion is possible. Entering
into the reality of the paschal mystery, which is at the heart of all
sacramental celebrations, is entering into the process of conversion and
transformation. It invites us to examine our relationships with God,
with other people, with ourselves, and with the world in order that
they might more authentically reflect the reality of God's presence.
We are challenged to be transformed so as to be sacraments — signs
of God's world of grace — to others.

This overview of Section One of Part Two makes clear the central
themes that shape the *Catechism*'s discussion of sacraments. Situating
the examination of sacraments within the broader context of liturgy
argues for the fundamental unity of the sacraments as expressions of
the one mystery of Christ. Rather than discrete, personal events,
sacramental celebrations invite the whole community to recognize and
celebrate God's presence in the world, God's present offer of grace.
Even while it is possible to separate out and examine the various components of sacramental rituals, their meaningfulness comes from their
contribution to the power of the ritual to point beyond itself to that
which it signifies.

It seems significant that the very last article of Section One of Part
Two returns us again to the fundamental connection among the sacraments and among the various expressions of sacramental celebrations.
The article "Liturgical Diversity and the Unity of the Mystery" highlights the unity that persists and is even strengthened as the liturgy
is given expression in different cultures. Rather than seeing this as a
threat to the unity of the one mystery of Christ, the text of the *Catechism* makes clear the contribution of such diversity:

> The mystery of Christ is so unfathomably rich that it can not be
> exhausted by its expression in any single liturgical tradition. . . .
> When the Churches lived their respective liturgical traditions in
> the communion of the faith and the sacraments of the faith, they
> enriched one another and grew in fidelity to Tradition and to the
> common mission of the whole Church (CCC 1201).

It is this principle of unity that we bring with us as we turn to Section
Two of Part Two with its exploration of the seven sacraments.

THE SEVEN SACRAMENTS

As we move into a discussion of the seven sacraments, the text, by necessity, becomes more specific in nature; here we look at each of the sacraments in some detail. The tendency, then, is for us to come to the *Catechism* with specific questions: What is the best order of initiation? What is the Church's teaching on intercommunion? What is the catechesis necessary for the celebration of reconciliation?, for example. We can tend to bring to this part of the *Catechism* specific pastoral questions in search of the answer. However, in light of the nature of catechisms discussed earlier in this text, it is clear that other types of questions might better guide our reading and reflection.

To the discussion in Section Two of Part Two of each of the sacraments, we might better bring questions such as these: How does the perspective presented in the *Catechism* give us added insight for engaging in the process of liturgical catechesis? What mind-set or worldview does the *Catechism* contribute to how we think about a particular sacramental situation? These questions can focus a reading of the *Catechism* so that the text acts to guide our thinking rather than to "solve" specific problems.

The length and detail of Section Two precludes a full analysis of the text here. However, with some of the central themes explored in Section One of Part Two as a backdrop, it is possible to make some comments concerning the general approach to the sacraments that shapes this section. One of the key considerations is how the material in Section One is reflected in Section Two's discussion of specific sacraments. We can explore these issues by considering the overall structure of Section Two, by applying the notion of liturgical catechesis to the approach used in this section, and by asking questions concerning the ecclesial nature of the sacraments.

Structure of Part Two

As discussed earlier in this chapter, the *Catechism* draws a sense of direction for its general discussion of the nature of sacraments from the documents of Vatican II, particularly the *Constitution on the Sacred Liturgy*. In that document, the sacraments are situated within the broader framework of liturgy; this perspective is evident in Section One of Part Two. Within that context, Eucharist is recognized as the premier sacrament, with the other sacraments seen in relationship to it (cf. SC 2,10 and CCC 1099, 1142, 1325). It is peculiar, then, that the structure of Section Two does not reflect that reality. Rather, it follows the classic lines of analogy to natural life borrowed from Thomas Aquinas and observed in the catechism from the Council of Trent, arranging the sacraments in order of initiation, healing and service to communion (CCC 1210-1211).

This sequence for presenting the sacraments has some advantages: it is a familiar one and many people have some sense of the rationale for this order. In addition, it has the potential for making clear that the sacraments play a role at every point of human development and are to be seen within that context.

But, the drawbacks to this schema are evident in Section Two. Without making clear the focal role of the Eucharist, the unity of the sacraments that is a central idea in Section One is diminished. The integrity of the seven sacraments, as expression of the one paschal mystery, is easily forgotten when the primary expression of that one mystery is not accentuated. While the *Catechism* does state that the Eucharist holds pride of place among the sacraments, the structure of Section Two presents a perspective that is less constructive for our understanding of sacraments.

In addition, the three-part structure of initiation — healing, service, communion — can easily result in a diminished perception of the role of Eucharist in the life of the Church. It is more than simply a source of sustenance, as the opening description of the chapter on the sacraments of initiation implies (CCC 1212). It certainly is that, but it is also a primary sacrament of healing and forgiveness; and to speak of "sacraments at the service of communion and the mission of the faithful" (CCC 1211) and not speak about the Eucharist seems like an anomaly.[11] While the discussion of Eucharist is in many ways informative, the role of Eucharist as the fundamental sacrament of the church is not as clearly set out as it could have been in a text of this nature.

The Model of Liturgical Catechesis

In the opening pages of Part Two, reference is made to the intimate connection between liturgy and catechesis. Liturgy is described as "the privileged place for catechizing the People of God" (CCC 1074). And liturgical catechesis as the process for initiating

> . . . people into the mystery of Christ by proceeding from the
> visible to the invisible, from the sign to the thing signified, from
> the "sacraments" to the "mysteries" (CCC 1075).

The *Catechism* states that this catechesis is called mystagogy. As the description of liturgical catechesis makes clear, the approach which is at the heart of mystagogy has, as its beginning point, the liturgical celebration. Mystagogy is, literally, a reflection on the mysteries or sacraments already celebrated.[12] One starts with the experience of the ritual and proceeds to explore the implications of the sacrament for our Christian teaching and practice.

Given this description of liturgical catechesis, it is surprising to note that the consistent structure used in the articles on the individual sacraments begins not with the ritual but with a discussion of doctrine. There is a basic format for the discussion of a sacrament: description of the sacrament, including some reference to its history; an explication of the rite itself; and a discussion of the recipient of the sacrament and the usual minister. Topics specific to a particular sacrament are set into this framework with a logic that is not always clear.[13]

The effect of this structure is to move the focus away from the sacramental ritual and, instead, highlight related doctrinal topics. In the article on marriage, for example, the description of the rite seems to be almost unrelated to the material around it, and the discussion moves quickly from the significance and power of the ritual to the necessary components for the form of marriage to be valid. Beginning the discussion of penance with a historical/doctrinal framework results in an emphasis on the individual's experience and the inference that individual celebration of the sacrament has primacy. There is little or no discussion of the role of the community in the celebration of the sacrament or the effect the sacrament has on the community's self-understanding. Both of these elements would surface by necessity if one were to engage in mystagogy in light of the experience of the various forms of the sacrament of penance.

Ecclesial Nature of the Sacraments

In Section One of Part Two, the *Catechism* again reflects the perspective of the *Constitution on the Sacred Liturgy* by making clear that it is the whole community of the baptized that celebrates sacramental liturgy (CCC 1140). A central theological perspective that supports this understanding of the community's role is also at the heart of the Vatican II document: that the Church itself is sacrament.[14] The lack of development of this idea in the *Catechism* becomes evident in the discussion of the individual sacraments. The Church is seen dispensing or granting the sacraments rather than attempting to express its own nature through the sacramental celebrations. This is played out in the discussion of the effects of the sacrament. The focus is first on the individual and only secondarily on the community or even on the individual's relationship with the community. For example, in discussing the effects of baptism the *Catechism* states: ''Thus the two principle effects are purification from sins and new birth in the Holy Spirit'' (CCC 1262). Only later does it make mention of the sacrament's role in incorporating the baptized into the Church or establishing the bonds of Christian unity.

The *Catechism*'s lack of development of the notion of the Church as sacrament has implications for how we understand the notion that the whole community of the baptized celebrates the sacramental liturgies.

As a resource for addressing specific liturgical/sacramental questions, Section Two has some real merit. As with the rest of the *Catechism*, the detailed references to Scripture, ecclesial documents, and early theologians provide guidance for further reading and reflection. However, the lack of integration within this section weakens its contribution to the process of constructing a synthesized understanding of sacraments and a sacramental understanding of ourselves and the Church.

SOME REMAINING ISSUES

As is evident in the discussion of Section Two, some problems exist in the presentation of the sacraments as set out in the *Catechism of the Catholic Church*. Here the concern is not disagreements concerning the theological perspective — it is always possible for conscientious theologians to differ on the emphasis a particular position received or the order in which ideas are presented. It is important however, to raise questions concerning the overall integrity of the *Catechism*'s presentation of the sacraments.

The first concern is discussed at length in the previous section: the apparent ''mismatch'' between Sections One and Two. The overall approach to the individual sacraments is often at odds with the description of sacramental events set out in Section One. This makes more emphatic the importance of reading the *Catechism* as a whole work. It is essential that the discussion of a particular sacrament be situated within the framework of the understanding of liturgy that is set out in the first section of Part Two.

A second issue concerns the different ways in which some classic theological concepts or terms are used within the text. One clear example of that is the use of the term "grace." The *Catechism* seems to go back and forth between a quantitative notion of grace and the sense of grace that supports a renewed understanding of sacraments: grace as divine life that is always and everywhere present. To speak of the sacraments as conferring or dispensing grace can promote a less helpful perspective on the meaning of grace and potentially foster a magical understanding of sacraments. Missing from this notion of grace is the reality argued for in the *Catechism:* God is always initiating and inviting us to relationship; before we act, God is present.

And, finally, a word about the "In Brief" sections. As is true throughout the *Catechism,* there are a number of places in Part Two where the summary statements correspond poorly with the article itself. The desire to bring into focus the complex realities inherent in the sacraments has lead in places to statements that are not adequately nuanced. One example of this is the description of the sacraments as "instituted by Christ" in the "In Brief" section (CCC 1131). In the text itself (CCC 1114-1116), this idea is carefully nuanced; the "In Brief" statement is susceptible to misinterpretation. In other contexts, the tenor of "In Brief" does not seem to match the section summarized. For example: in the final article of Section One, "Liturgical Diversity and the Unity of the Mystery," the emphasis seems to be on the rich contribution that the diverse expression of the Christian mystery can make to the whole Church. There is with this the recognition of the importance of unity. In the "In Brief" section, the emphasis is not so much on the contribution of diversity but on the requirement of unity. While the "In Brief" sections may be helpful guides in reading the full text, caution must be used when they are cited out of the context of the whole.

PART TWO: CONTRIBUTION AND CHALLENGE

What role can Part Two, "The Celebration of the Christian Mystery," play in the ongoing process of catechesis on the sacraments? How does the discussion in these pages enhance the sacramental life of the Church and our ability to reflect upon it? How is this text of help to the catechist? I believe that Part Two makes a number of significant contributions and leaves us with some challenging tasks.

The overall theme of Part Two is that the sacraments are part of a wider reality and need to be understood within the context of the liturgy. By situating the sacraments in that broader framework, catechists are invited to recognize the fundamental unity of the sacramental events and their significance to the Church's self-understanding. The attention for catechesis shifts from details around a particular sacrament to the process of initiating people into a sacramental understanding of the Church and the world. Formation for the celebration of sacraments emphasizes a heightening of the community's awareness of God's action. Given the framework provided by Section One of Part Two, the focus of catechesis is not so much the ritual but the reality to which it points: the relationship with one's self and others that is characterized by the always present offer of God's grace.

But in those insights about the nature of liturgical or sacramental catechesis rests the challenge inherent in the process of conveying the *Catechism*'s content concerning the seven sacraments. The question at the heart of sacramental formation is not ''How do I prepare this group to celebrate this specific sacrament?'' but ''How does this group become more connected to the Church's liturgical life as it enhances our awareness of God's presence?'' The challenge is to connect those who are preparing to celebrate a sacrament with the experience to which the sacrament points. To do that, the catechist must come to Section Two with an understanding of Section One, and with an awareness of the experience of the faith community firmly in mind.

In Section One it is made clear that liturgical catechesis is fundamentally mystagogical; the beginning place is the experience of the ritual itself and the awareness of the reality of God's presence to which the ritual points. While the information presented in the various articles in Section Two is helpful to the catechist's understanding of a particular sacrament, the lens through which catechesis for sacraments is best viewed, and through which information about a sacrament is interpreted, is the faith experience of the community and the rituals which give expression to that experience.

At the core of the Church's reality is its sacramental life, a key expression of which are the seven sacraments. As liturgical events, the sacraments invite us to participate in the saving action of God, in the paschal mystery. As identity-shaping rituals, the sacraments help us name our understanding of who we are as a Church gathered in the name of Jesus Christ. As catechetical moments, the sacraments evoke our reflections upon our individual and communal memory of God's action in human history and challenge us to continue to live lives reflective of that divine presence. Even with its inevitable shortcomings, Section Two of the *Catechism* provides an important point of entry into the dynamic realities called sacraments.

For Further Reading

A wide range of topics has been explored in this chapter. While the notes provide insights into the sources that shape my thinking, this bibliographical essay is designed to complement the information provided in the notes and to give direction for further reading in the basic area of sacrament and liturgy.

Since the perspective reflected in the *Constitution on the Sacred Liturgy* contributed significantly to the fundamental perspective of Section One of Part Two, commentaries on that document can provide further insight to reading the *Catechism*. Two that were published at the time of the council continue to be helpful: Louis Bouyer, *The Liturgy Revived: A Doctrinal Commentary on the Conciliar Constitution on the Liturgy* (Notre Dame: University of Notre Dame Press, 1964) and A. Bugnini and C. Braga, ed. *The Commentary on the Constitution and on the Instruction on the Sacred Liturgy*, trans. V.P. Mallon. (New York: Benziger, 1965). More current commentary is provided by the collection of essays in "Part IV: Liturgy and Sacraments" in R. Latourelle, ed. *Vatican II: Assessment and Perspectives Twenty-five Years After*, vol. 2 (New York: Paulist, 1989). From a specifically American perspective, see the essay by Kevin W. Irwin in Timothy O'Connell, ed. *Vatican II and Its Documents: An American Reappraisal*, Theology and Life Series, vol 15. (Wilmington, Del.: Glazier, 1986).

The collection of essays in Michael Downey and Richard Fragomeni, *A Promise of Presence* (Washington, D.C.: Pastoral Press, 1992), explores some of the fundamental issues in contemporary liturgical studies. Kevin Irwin, *Context and Text: Method in Liturgical Theology* (Collegeville, Minn.: The Liturgical Press, 1994) examines sacraments from the perspective of liturgical theology.

Resources that serve as the important bridge between insights of liturgical study and pastoral expression include Gabe Huck, *Liturgy with Style and Grace* (Chicago: Liturgical Training Publications, 1984). The brief essays on a wide range of liturgical and pastoral concern are helpful for those working to give expression to the convictions about the nature of liturgy that flow from the *Constitution on the Sacred Liturgy* and other subsequent Church documents.

The seven-volume series published under the title *Alternative Futures for Worship* (Collegeville, Minn.: The Liturgical Press, 1987) is a collection of essays that bring into dialogue the multiple perspectives from which to examine the sacraments. "Volume I: General Introduction" contains helpful essays by Michael Cowan, Paul Philibert, and Edward Kilmartin.

It is impossible to survey the plethora of books written concerning the sacraments in general and each of the seven sacraments. Here I simply wish to cite those books which contribute to my own thinking and those which might be helpful for further reading. Bibliographies in these books can direct the reader interested in exploring a specific sacrament in depth.

Several books describe the historical development of the sacraments. Among the more detailed is Joseph Martos, *Doors to the Sacred: A Historical Introduction to Sacraments in the Catholic Church*, expanded edition (Tarrytown, N.Y.: Triumph Books, 1991). The more recent edition includes updated bibliographies. Most readers will find William Bausch, *A New Look at the Sacraments* (Mystic, Conn.: Twenty-Third Publications, 1983) a highly accessible discussion of historical and pastoral issues related to sacraments.

For a well integrated presentation on the nature of sacraments and their role in the Church, one can hardly do better than two small books by Karl Rahner. *The Church and the Sacraments* (London: Burns and Oates, 1963) and *Meditation on the Sacraments* (New York: Seabury Press 1974). A synthesis of the insights of Rahner and other theologians is provided in Kenan B. Osborne, *Sacramental Theology: A General Introduction* (New York: Paulist, 1988).

Two other books on the sacraments attempt to draw the connection between sacramental theology and insights from other disciplines. Michael Downey, *Clothed in Christ: The Sacraments and Christian Living* (New York: Crossroad, 1987) provides a good introduction to sacramental theology and draws out the ethical implications of the sacraments. Robert L. Browning and Roy A Reed *The Sacraments in Religious Educa-*

tion and Liturgy (Birmingham, Ala.: Religious Education Press, 1985) examines fundamental concepts of ritual, sign, and symbol and examines the relationship among liturgy, sacraments, and religious education.

Notes for Chapter 5

1. All quotations from the documents of Vatican Council II are taken from *Vatican Council II: The Conciliar and Post Conciliar Documents*, 1981 Edition, Austin Flannery, ed. (Northport, N.Y.: Costello Publishing, 1980).

2. For a concise summary of the liturgical movement, see "Liturgical Movement" and "History of Liturgical Reform" in Peter Fink, ed., *The New Dictionary of Sacramental Worship* (Collegeville, Minn.: The Liturgical Press, 1990). Two books that provide insight into the people behind the movement are Robert L. Tuzik, ed., *How Firm a Foundation: Leaders of the Liturgical Movement* (Chicago: Liturgy Training Publications, 1990) and Kathleen Hughes, ed., *How Firm a Foundation: Voices of the Early Liturgical Movement* (Chicago: Liturgy Training Publications, 1990). The first consists of short biographical sketches of persons who shaped the liturgical movement; Hughes's book contains excerpts from the writing and speaking of some of these leaders.

3. One of the most articulate voices of the essential connection between the liturgical movement and the renewal of catechesis is Josef Jungmann. The relationship between liturgy and catechesis is made clear in two of Jungmann's key catechetical texts: *The Good News Yesterday and Today* (New York: Sadlier, 1962) and *Handing on the Faith: A Manual of Catechetics* (New York: Herder and Herder, 1959). In this country, that relationship between liturgy and catechetical renewal can be seen in the work and influence of Virgil Michel, O.S.B. For an examination of the fundamental connection among liturgy, catechesis, and social justice that shaped Michel's work, see R.W. Franklin and Robert Spaeth, *Virgil Michel: American Catholic* (Collegeville, Minn.: The Liturgical Press, 1988). The extensive bibliographical essay included in the text guides the reader to the primary source material.

4. For a description of the structure and content of the *Constitution on the Sacred Liturgy*, see A. Hasting, *The Concise Guide to the Documents of the Second Vatican Council*, vol. 1 (London: Darton, Longman and Todd, 1968) 109–113. See the Bibliographical Essay at the conclusion of this chapter for further reading on the *Constitution on the Sacred Liturgy*.

5. The significance of these shifts in the core focus to how sacraments are perceived is discussed in a number of texts on the sacraments. See, for example, Michael Downey, *Clothed in Christ: The Sacraments and Christian Living* (New York: Crossroad, 1987) 8–17; he connects these shifts to movements in fundamental elements of Christology, ecclesiology, and Christian anthropology. Robert L. Browning and Roy A Reed. *The Sacraments in Religious Education and Liturgy* (Birmingham, Alabama, 1985) set out a series of movements that highlight the significance of the "quiet revolution in sacramental understanding," see 3–16.

6. Further discussion of "symbols" and the power of symbols in the sacramental system can be found in the catechism (CCC 1145-1152); this is discussed later in this chapter.

7. For a discussion of the significance of the concept of the Church as sacrament, see Kenan B. Osborne, *Sacramental Theology: A General Introduction* (New York: Paulist, 1988) 86–99.

8. Karl Rahner, *Meditation on the Sacraments* (New York: Seabury Press, 1974) xi.

9. Karl Rahner, "Reflections on the Experience of Grace," in *Theological Investigations III*, trans. C. Ernst (Baltimore: Helicon Press, 1961) 87.

10. This may be one way to understand the Church's teaching concerning the necessity, for believers, of the sacraments for salvation (CCC 1129). Participation in the sacraments is a formal affirmation of God's grace; active refusal to participate can be a negation of that offer.

11. For a fuller discussion of the presentation of the Eucharist in *Catechism of the Catholic Church*, see Peter E. Fink, "The Liturgy and Eucharist in the Catechism," *The Universal Catechism Reader: Reflections and Responses*, ed. Thomas J. Reese (San Francisco: Harper and Row, 1990) 95–108. While Fink's analysis is based on the first draft of the *Catechism*, I believe many of his comments are applicable to the final version as well.

12. The clearest example for this is the catechesis connected with the Order of Christian Initiation of Adults. This is described in RCIA, nn. 244–246.

13. For further discussion of this, see David Power's discussion on the first draft of the catechism in "The Sacraments in the Catechism," *The Universal Catechism Reader*, 113–116.

14. The idea of the Church as sacrament is spoken about, in passing, in a few places in the catechism, but is not developed. See CCC 1118 and 1142.

CHAPTER 6

Life in Christ

Timothy Backous, O.S.B.

There can be no doubt that the much anticipated English version of the *Catechism of the Catholic Church* will be enthusiastically welcomed by those who find the current state of the Church's morality in a "crisis." Feelings of joy and relief at even the announcement of such a publication suggest an expectation of clarity and conciseness worthy of its predecessors. But Cardinal Joseph Ratzinger warns against such expectations, especially in regard to Part Three of the *Catechism*, "Life in Christ." In an interview with *Trenta Giorni,* he said:

> . . . anyone who says that the catechism is a list of sins is gravely mistaken. . . . Less than a third of the text regards morality, presented within the great context of the history of God and humanity and of the revelation of God, who also offers himself in the bodily concreteness of the sacraments in the communion of the church.[1]

The element of context is critical to those who approach Part Three of the *Catechism*. Cardinal Ratzinger rightly warns that the "bottom line" is not whether the Church still considers certain sins a moral offense but that we understand *why* these actions are wrong and *how* the Church arrived at these conclusions. Moreover, to be a source of encouragement and hope, the *Catechism*'s presentation of morality must take on a more positive tone.

In the interview cited earlier, Ratzinger continues his discussion of Part Three, "Life in Christ":

> This section of the text is not a list of sins but is aimed at illustrating how moral living is constituted within a Christian perspective. Morality thus becomes a very simple thing: it is friendship with the Lord; it is living and journeying with Him.[2]

Friendship with the Lord is an appropriate way to describe the reality of our moral life. We understand the expectations, the commitment, and the fidelity it takes to build and sustain human relationships. So much more, then, can be said for our relationship with God, which is brought to life in a very concrete way in the person of Jesus Christ. We have been called to share the gifts of God. When we say "yes" to that call, then our moral lives must take the shape of that response. Since God is always faithful no matter how far we fall short, the moral teachings of the Church are a constant reminder for us to return to the path of righteousness and once again strive for holiness.

Part Three seeks to explore and define the Church's moral teaching for a new age. Clarification and explanation are an integral part of our search for the truth, but there is a new dimension reflected in this particular catechism: the Church encourages us — even demands — that we not examine our moral life as a separate entity divorced from all other aspects of our faith. When we say we "believe," we are saying much more than "I am willing to obey these commandments." In the spirit of Vatican II, the *Catechism* helps us make those connections by presenting a "summary" of our faith in a more holistic way.

The *Catechism* makes it quite clear that this is not a task done in isolation. "No one can believe alone, just as no one can live alone. You have not given faith to yourself as you have not given yourself life" (CCC 166). As members of society, we strive together to establish a way of life that benefits all people. The gifts of freedom and rights are meant for the common good. When we fall short of that aim, society has ways of righting the wrong. Likewise, as members of the Church we have a concern not only for our own well-being, but for the common good. Our moral sense comes from the community, so it is only appropriate for our moral actions to benefit that community.

SOME PROMINENT THEMES IN PART THREE

The spirit of Vatican II emphasized the notion of community, and it is no accident that the *Catechism* relies heavily upon the council's thinking. Of the 343 citations in the section on morality, a significant number of them refer to *Gaudium et Spes* (GS) or "The Church in the Modern World."[3] This document was an effort to define the Catholic tradition in light of the modern age and those elements that help and hinder the Church's mission. In it, humanity is described as "the meeting point of many conflicting forces'' (GS 9). Our sinfulness causes anxiety, while our mastery of technology and nature nudge us toward repudiation of our creature status. We end up doing the very things we know we should not do. This struggle is a constant one, and the council fathers are quick to point out that in spite of our many accomplishments, the world is no happier. As we sort out the complexities of the material world, we seem to slip further and further away from the paradise it promises.

The Church, if it is fulfilling its mission, is the beacon of light in the midst of a world that is misled by its own self-confidence. Constantly calling us back to Jesus Christ, the Church reminds us that service, not mastery, is the vocation of all human life. By virtue of our membership in the Body of Christ, our highest aspirations must center on the building of God's kingdom, not our own.

The *Catechism* is an effort to bring proper focus back to our moral tradition. Because the Church is not working in a spirit of crisis that has colored past efforts in formulating our teachings, Part Three has a fresh and creative aura about it. It is the logical step forward from the solid foundations set down by Vatican II, in which all believers are called to rebirth and renewal. Certain themes, like the common good, that permeated the council's teachings, are very much evident in Part Three and demonstrate the close connection of the *Catechism* and *Gaudium et Spes*. To treat all of these themes would require volumes, so we will focus on six of them that represent the strongest ties between the council's thought and that of the authors of Part Three.

THEME ONE: "WE ARE MADE IN THE IMAGE AND LIKENESS OF GOD"[4]

> Christian, recognize your dignity and, now that you share in God's own nature, do not return by sin to your former base condition by sinning. Remember who is your head and of whose body you are a member. Never forget that you have been rescued from the power of darkness and brought into the light of the Kingdom of God (CCC 1691).

These ancient words of St. Leo the Great provide the backdrop against which all the other major principles of this section are examined. It is a crucial reference point because the tendency is to cast our response to God's call in negative terms. The *Catechism* tries to reenergize our morality by focusing less on what we must *not* do and instead on who we are: God's children and members of the Body of Christ. In baptism, human beings share "in the light and power of the divine spirit" (CCC 1704). God reveals the fullness of what it means to be human in the life, death and resurrection of Jesus. We are no less than the image of God that "shines forth in communion of persons, in the likeness of the union of the divine persons among themselves" (CCC 1702).

This theme is important because it reminds us of our dignity as baptized Christians and also underlines the purpose of God's creating us: to embody the light of God's goodness so that it may shine in the world. To say we are made in the image of God, then, is not simply a way of understanding the order of creation; it says something about the very basis of our existence. We are created to love and serve God through each other. This is not the end point of the moral life but the very beginning. We seek good and avoid evil because of this dignity.

THEME TWO: "SIN IS THE ABUSE OF FREEDOM"[5]

The underlying principles of our moral tradition affirm that our entire existence is a gift from God. Consequently, this is where the *Catechism* begins its "contextualizing." That we are created by God means that we are essentially "of God" or even "god-like."

The optimism in Part Three of the *Catechism* is obvious without being unrealistic. While we can rejoice with confidence that we are God's children, a superficial glance at our world is a firm reminder that we have a long journey ahead of us toward perfection. Humanity, as blessed and gifted as it is, remains broken and wounded by sin. We do not act as we ought and, as a result, constantly find ourselves missing the mark or wandering off the path of righteousness.

Sin is real and the Church's moral tradition has long held that we, through knowledge and reflection, can define and articulate what benefits the common good and what harms it. This has not always been an easy task, because our knowledge and intellect constantly urge us to rethink and reevaluate what we consider to be sinful. Nevertheless, the Church is guided by the Holy Spirit and our moral reflection depends on that guidance, even in the midst of shifting or changing opinions. What is most important is that we have firmly dedicated ourselves to a faithfulness that rejects sin. Sin is not "of God" or God's kingdom. It is "an utterance, a deed, or a desire contrary to the eternal law" (CCC 1849). Therefore, it has no place in our lives.

Sin affects our attempt to be perfect as God is perfect. Human nature, though created in love to be holy, is too often steered away from its final goal. For this reason, we turn to God for help in the person of Jesus. The Son of God is the fulfillment of the law, and that means grace, the "free and undeserved help that God gives us" (CCC 1996), is available to sustain our efforts to do good and avoid evil. Jesus is the way to the Father, and so as disciples we follow his example, we listen to his words, and we give thanks in his memory. "The moral law finds its fullness and its unity in Christ" (CCC 1953).

THEME THREE: "THE ESSENTIAL NATURE OF HUMANITY"[6]

> Man is not deceived when he regards himself as superior to bodily things and as more than just a speck of nature or a nameless unit in the city of man. For by his power to know himself in the depths of his being, he rises above the whole universe of mere objects (GS 14).

Deep in the heart of every human being is a voice that calls us to holiness and happiness. It is that voice which makes it possible for us to yearn for doing good and avoiding evil. This vocation or "calling" is the invitation of God who created us to be happy, and our moral lives are the working response to it. Thus we are, by our very nature, seekers of "beatitude." The *Catechism* says that the desire for beatitude is a natural one of divine order. God has placed that desire within the human heart in order to draw us "to the One who alone can fill it" (CCC 1718).

The *Catechism* insists that all Christian morality rests on this call to happiness. "Such beatitude surpasses the understanding and power" of human beings (CCC 1722). It is God's free gift. The essence of human nature, therefore, is truly an exalted one because it strives for a happiness that is not earthly but divine. Christian morality teaches us that "true happiness [resides] . . . in God alone, the source of every good and of all love" (CCC 1723).

THEME FOUR: "THE DIGNITY OF THE MORAL CONSCIENCE"

One of most familiar passages of *Gaudium et Spes* deals with the nature of conscience. It is our "most secret core," our "inner sanctuary" (GS 16). There we are alone with God, and it is in the conscience that we freely express our love of God and neighbor or reject them both. Of all the terminology used to define our moral life, conscience remains one of the most complex. Timothy O'Connell has gone to great lengths in helping us understand just what we mean by the word "conscience."[7] He proposes that there are three senses in our tradition: conscience as an ability or capacity, conscience as a process of reflection, and conscience as an actual decision or judgment. It is the third sense that most readily comes to mind when we use the term, because most of us think of conscience as that "inner voice" we hear when faced with making a difficult decision. As a capacity that is part of our created nature and gift from God, our conscience becomes a sort of inner judge, weighing facts, considering options, and then rendering a decision.

But the other two senses are no less critical in forming a complete understanding of conscience. In order for us to even hope to hear God's voice and discover God's will for us in this life, we must have that ability in the first place. It is part of the human blueprint that draws us toward the good and away from evil. God's law could not touch the human heart otherwise.

The second sense of conscience is equally important. It refers to that aspect of our inner selves which "processes" our moral reality. We are constantly seeking good and avoiding evil if our conscience has been properly formed. This function of conscience, then, is our way of reevaluating what is good and evil and assessing our own behavior in light of new insight and deeper conversion. What was not thought sinful to former generations (slavery, for example) is now considered gravely sinful. Conversely, what was once considered gravely sinful to our forebears, may not seem as serious to us given contemporary insights about human beings and their relationships with one another.

"A human being must always obey the certain judgment of his conscience" (CCC 1790). The *Catechism* makes clear that we condemn ourselves if we deliberately act against our conscience's judgment. Conscience has dignity because it is there that we assume full responsibility for our own moral lives. Ultimately, we cannot claim virtue or innocence because someone told us to do this or avoid that. Our conscience is an "inner sanctuary" where we meet God face to face. Amazingly, the dignity of conscience is not lost even when it goes astray. Though we are continually enjoined to follow our conscience, we must also be aware that it can be misinformed or led astray. By virtue of its authority to teach, the Church provides direction. It is our responsibility to inform our conscience accordingly. The "bottom line" is that ". . . a good and pure conscience is enlightened by true faith" (CCC 1794). The faith we speak of is that which comes to us as members of the believing community; therefore, conscience formation is not an individual pursuit but a communal one. For this reason, the *Catechism* sees the Church's instruction and guidance as essential to the process.

THEME FIVE: "SOCIAL JUSTICE"[8]

Gaudium et Spes makes clear the need for the Church to address modern issues.

> At all times the Church carries the responsibility of reading the signs of the time and of interpreting them in the light of the Gospel, if it is to carry out its task. In language intelligible to every generation, she should be able to answer the ever recurring questions which men ask about the meaning of this present life and of the life to come, and how one is related to the other. We must be aware of and understand the aspirations, the yearning and the often dramatic features of the world in which we live (GS 4).

One such "aspiration" is the fight for social justice and equality. The equal dignity of all human beings makes demands on us to "strive for fairer and more humane conditions" (GS 29). The scandal of social and economic disparity challenges the Church to speak out prophetically against injustice wherever it may be manifested.

The *Catechism* repeats the call for social justice that has echoed through the centuries.

> Respect for the human person proceeds by way of respect for the principle that "everyone should look on his neighbor (without any exception) as 'another self,' above all bearing in mind his life and the means necessary for living it with dignity" (GS 27). No legislation could by itself do away with the fears, prejudices, and attitudes of pride and selfishness which obstruct the establishment of truly fraternal societies. Such behavior will only cease through the charity that finds in each person a "neighbor" . . . (CCC 1931).

This theme, that of our neighbor as being "another self," is yet more evidence of the deeply theological nature of this section on morality. It seems we are growing more aware of the need to change from within rather than trying to legislate change from without. Laws that protect the rights of others are rendered useless if the human heart cannot see any real connection to our neighbor.

The need to make this connection becomes even more urgent, says the *Catechism,* when it involves the disadvantaged (CCC 1932). The essence of the Christian response for bringing about social justice, then, has to do with a concern for any human being who is lacking dignity, freedom, and temporal or spiritual goods. While it may be necessary to create social institutions that safeguard these basic goods, our concern for each other must first be born and nurtured in each individual heart.

THEME SIX: "THE NEED TO TRANSCEND AN INDIVIDUALISTIC MORALITY"[9]

Ever since Vatican II called for a renewal of moral theology, the Church has been struggling to rearticulate what we believe about right and wrong without being overly legalistic. Being moral goes far beyond just obeying rules. It is also more than "not doing" something. It means conversion and responsibility, which leads to a greater awareness of and sensitivity to the common good. The council envisioned a renewed sense of moral attentiveness that would be brought to life in a concrete commitment to the well-being of society as a whole.

> Let everyone consider it [their] sacred duty to count social obligations among [humanity's] chief duties today and observe them as such. For the more closely the world comes together, the more do [human beings'] obligations transcend particular groups and gradually extend to the whole world. This will be realized only if individuals and groups practice moral and social virtues and foster them in social living. Then, under the necessary help of divine grace, there will arise a generation of [people], the molders of a new humanity (GS 30).

An effort to keep the common good at front and center stage of our moral reflection has met with varying degrees of success over the centuries. As morality became more closely associated with canon law, the Church tended to lose sight of morality's overall goal: to love one another as Jesus Christ commanded us to do. As the Church moved through years of growth and crisis, there were tendencies to emphasize individual moral "performance" rather than the common good. By concentrating on the rightness and wrongness of actions, the moral tradition was weighed down by legalistic argumentation. The purpose of being moral had more to do with personal righteousness and less with service to the Body of Christ.

The *Catechism* reminds us that our personal moral life is not an end in and of itself but merely sets the stage for our service to the common good, which includes three essential elements:

> Respect for and promotion of the fundamental rights of the person; prosperity, or development of the spiritual and temporal goods of society; the peace and security of the group and its members (CCC 1925).

Gaudium et Spes states that "the order of things must be subordinated to the order of persons, and not the other way around" (GS 26). Therefore, the common good is always "oriented toward the progress of persons" (CCC 1912). Such an order, the *Catechism* goes on to say, "is founded on truth, built up in justice and animated by love" (CCC 1912). This reaffirmation of the common good, for too long unnoticed in our moral tradition, provides the foundation on which the Church can explore, reflect, and then formulate moral norms.[10]

The Church believes itself capable of establishing concrete teachings that give substance to the theological and philosophical principles upon which they rest. Morality can never be just "heady musing." Our abstract thinking, though important to our ongoing search for truth, must at some point give way to practical application. Unfortunately, for many Catholics, this process has seemed too cold, too legal, and too distant from the complexity and ambiguity of human experience. Rarely do we feel anymore that right and wrong are easily defined. A renewed emphasis on the common good in our moral teaching moves us away from questions that begin "Is it a sin to . . . ?" and closer to the real questions we should be asking about our Christian responsibility, like "What do my thoughts and actions contribute to the common good?"

From the earliest beginnings, the Church has tried to shepherd its people by articulating, as clearly as possible, what is expected from someone who says "I believe." Recently, we have come to appreciate how each generation must meet this difficult challenge in the wake of changing social norms, increased human understanding, and shifts in theological and philosophical thought. For example, modern theology seems to stress that God is not distant from us but, in fact, just the opposite: God is alive in our hearts. This shift will naturally affect the way we flesh out our morality. If the image of God is fearsome and distant, then our response seems best expressed in terms of obedience. However, if we use the image of God as creator, as "Abba," or as "Sustainer" for the way we think about God, then our morality becomes a response to that creative love. In other words, we are not people of fear but of love.

FROM PRINCIPLE TO PRAXIS

The second section of "Life in Christ" describes how we make concrete our love for one another and God. Like the young man who approaches Jesus and asks what he must do to obtain eternal life, we too are searching for ways to make belief come to life in our everyday lives. And to us, like the young man, Jesus says "If you wish to enter into life, observe the commandments" (Matt 19:16-19). His response attests to the perennial stature of the Ten Commandments in the Judeo-Christian tradition. They remain a central focus of the Church's desire to help its believers live out a commitment to their faith.

This help has been articulated as God's law, which dwells in our hearts and has found expression throughout history. Moses received this law from God in the form of ten "words" or commandments. He led the Israelites from slavery to freedom so that God's law could come alive in their fidelity to Yahweh's covenant. Their journey set the stage for the new law of the gospel, which completes and brings to fulfillment the old law. It does this by underlining the essence of our covenantal relationship to God — love. Love is God's motivation in creating us and calling us "good." Therefore, to love one another is quite simply to obey our nature. Jesus taught this law with insistence and without compromise. It is not just a matter of being nice to one another. Nor is it merely a suggestion. It is a command to follow the law written in our hearts. We must love if we long to be fully human. We must love if we claim to be followers of Christ.

This law of love is the light by which the *Catechism of the Catholic Church* examines the Ten Commandments. Jesus did not abolish the old law but rather fulfilled it. For this reason, the commandments remain the backbone of our moral tradition and provide us with a clear set of expectations that any community of love must obey. They are the concrete application of the underlying principles that shape our morality.

It is important to note that in light of the principles set forth in Section One of "Life in Christ," the commandments take on added significance because of their concern for the common good. The God of Israel is the God of the covenant, a covenant made with a community. Therefore, it is within the community that we hear these "words," and it is for the good of the community that we "obey" them.

> The gift of the commandments of the Law is part of the covenant God sealed with his own. In Exodus, the revelation of the "ten words" is granted between proposal of the covenant and its conclusion — after the people had committed themselves to "do" all that the Lord had said, and to "obey" it (CCC 2060).

The community's striving for perfection is "a *response* to the Lord's loving initiative. It is the acknowledgement and homage given to God and a worship of thanksgiving. It is cooperation with the plan God pursues in history" (CCC 2062).

Since the Ten Commandments express the tangible way in which we are called to serve God and neighbor, it is no surprise that the first three refer specifically to God and the last seven to neighbor. The *Catechism* reminds us, though, that the Decalogue

> . . . forms a coherent whole. Each "word" refers to each of the others and to all of them. . . . To transgress one commandment is to infringe all the others. One cannot honor another person without blessing God his Creator (CCC 2069).

In the same section, the *Catechism* goes on to say that one cannot worship God without loving all humans as God's creatures. The Ten Commandments serve as a source of unity for our relationship with God and with one another (CCC 2069).

In its attempt to clarify the "specifics" of Catholic morality, Section Two of "Life in Christ" does not compromise the complexity of this task. Whenever we move from theory to practice, from principle to praxis, there are bound to be difficulties. St. Thomas Aquinas insisted that when we move from the general to the specific regarding moral norms, we must then take into account all the many factors regarding human beings and their actions.[11] Considerations such as freedom, intent, knowledge, will, and particular circumstances must be figured into the evaluative process. Although the Church teaches that there are some actions which are always wrong regardless of who does them and why they are done, for the most part, our moral assessment relies upon many factors other than just the act itself.[12]

SOME CONTEMPORARY ISSUES

While the ideas presented in Part Three of the *Catechism* help the Church articulate a summary of its moral teachings, there is still room for further refinement of these teachings. Three concerns deserve particular attention. The first is that this text tends to be "act-centered" and not "person-centered" when it comes to evaluating moral issues. Secondly, it appears the *Catechism* is unwilling to affirm the Church's openness to the world (an attitude fostered by Vatican II) and instead, takes the form of "internal legislation." A third concern is that the updated text emphasizes obedience rather than responsibility. It is to these issues we now turn.

ACT-CENTERED OR PERSON-CENTERED

Since Vatican II, the Church's approach to moral teaching has undergone a subtle yet remarkable transformation. With the documents created by the council, we have begun to center our moral teachings on the person rather than the act.[13] Evident in numerous documents, including *Humanae Vitae*, this change is rooted primarily in our updated knowledge and modern appreciation of the natural law.[14] Our tradition firmly holds that God's will is stamped on creation and that we have within us the ability to define and understand the particulars of that law. In this sense we share in God's wisdom; we are able to orient our lives and our actions toward what is good. "The natural law expresses the original moral sense" that makes it possible for us to recognize good from evil (CCC 1954). This "discernment" process is what gives us the confidence to set down concrete moral norms. Relying on this certainty, we can determine which actions are right and which are wrong.

With our ever-increasing appreciation for the complexity of human beings and the world in which we live, more questions are being raised regarding the natural law as a sure guide in moral evaluation. Is the natural law unchangeable? Is human nature unchangeable? If so, are the applications of the natural law also unchangeable? The *Catechism* upholds the firm stance that the natural law "is *immutable* and permanent throughout the variations of history" (CCC 1958), yet "applications of the natural law varies greatly; it can demand reflection that takes account of various conditions of life according to places, times and circumstances" (CCC 1957). It would seem then, that this particular *Catechism* urges great care when we begin our evaluation with the act itself. Time, place, and circumstance must be considered in the process.

Even more compelling is the concern for the human person as the starting point of any moral assessment. Rather than simply address the "matter" of sin, we must first remember that our primary concern is how this action affects an individual and the community. What do factors such as time, place, and circumstances tell us about this person? By focusing on the physical act and its ramifications, we may be overlooking something more important: the effects of that sin.

One particular area that is mentioned in the *Catechism* which highlights this concern is that of social sin. No longer can we be sure that a certain act is not sinful just because it is not specifically dealt with. In its treatment of the commandment, "You shall not steal," the second section of Part Three expands the notion of "acting" to include a participation in and support of social structures that oppress, wound, or even steal from members of society. As Christians, we have a grave responsibility to promote peace and justice. The thrust of this teaching does not seem to emphasize certain acts as much as it warns against attitudes or apathy that may bring about sinful results.[15]

Some critics of the *Catechism* have argued that its teaching on sexual ethics is not as successful in moving away from an "act-centered" approach. There is little in the text, says Lawrence Cunningham, that "provides . . . consolation to the divorced and remarried beyond telling them to be faithful to the Church while denying them access to the Communion rail."[16] Likewise, a rather straightforward mention of "intrinsically evil" acts seems to provide little in the way of broader consideration for time, place, and circumstance.

> There are acts which, in and of themselves, independently of circumstances and intentions, are always gravely illicit by reason of

their object; such as blasphemy, perjury, murder and adultery (CCC 1756).

It is the opinion of some contemporary theologians that this approach is too fixed and that more openness to uncertainty is in order.[17]

OPENNESS TO THE WORLD

Related to this is the criticism that Part Three explores and clarifies our moral tradition without paying enough attention to the voices outside the Church. *Gaudium et Spes* clearly states that our efforts to renew the Church cannot be done in isolation. We cannot retreat to an inner room and pull down all the shades in order to discover who we are and what we believe.

> [The Church] is convinced that there is a considerable and varied help that it can receive from the world in preparing the ground for the gospel, both from individuals and society as a whole, by their talents and activities (GS 40).

Much of this reliance on outside voices has to do with a sincere effort to promote ecumenism, but in the wake of more recent realities (including the realm of medical ethics), the Church has discovered a necessity to learn from scientific data that in some cases has a direct bearing on the way we morally assess certain issues. The entire debate on artificial contraception, for example, is just one instance of the Church's desire to consult and consider the opinions of those experts outside the realm of theology and doctrine.

The trend continues to this very day and has been responsible for the significant revision of some key issues. Homosexuality, for one, has been a concern of the Church for quite some time. Even though the *Catechism* clearly states that "homosexual persons are called to chastity" (CCC 2359), it also makes a distinction between orientation and activity, calls us to compassion, respect, and sensitivity for those who struggle with it, and warns that discrimination toward the homosexual is to be avoided (CCC 2358).

Part Three's treatment of masturbation is also shaded by more current information which seems to suggest that it may not be as grave a problem as once thought. Though still considered a "grave offense" by the Church primarily because it is "a deliberate use of the sexual faculty outside of normal marital relations," the text cautions us:

To form an equitable judgment about the subject's moral responsibility and to guide pastoral action, one must take into account the affective immaturity, force of acquired habit, conditions of anxiety, or other psychological or social factors that lessen or even extenuate moral culpability (CCC 2352).

This assessment is a far cry from the "absolutism" of former documents that more or less decried the act as an offense against the natural law and based its teaching on incomplete scientific information.

The reliance upon outside voices is not only evident in the revised teaching of "old" issues. The very fact that this catechism specifically mentions "new" sins, such as tax evasion, drunken driving, and the unjust treatment of animals, indicates a new awareness of the dimensions of sin in our world and how our moral responsibility as Catholics extends far beyond the sexual realm.

OBEDIENCE AND RESPONSIBILITY

Finally, in Section Two, Part Three, there is the issue of "obedience versus responsibility." Although this is a bit more academic in nature, the argument raises some important concerns. William Spohn, reacting to the first draft of the text says that

> The language of law dominates the fundamental moral vision of the catechism just as it did in moral theology following the Council of Trent. A more adult ethic sees the moral life as taking responsibility for discovering humane solutions to problems of the personal and social life.[18]

Spohn's uneasiness with the "forensic" nature of the text was shared by the Administrative Committee of the United States Catholic Conference who felt that "the moral vision [of the catechism] was couched in terms of obedience to divine law rather than the following of Christ."[19]

Francis J. Buckley, S.J., echoes this point of view in claiming that

> Catechesis should bring faith to maturity. This maturity involves the whole person, intellect, will, emotions, and habits. It includes conviction and action. But [the catechism] does not nourish and deepen faith, leading to deeper love of God and others. Its approach is too dry, too rational, too cold.[20]

He goes on to say that the Church deserves better than this. The *Catechism*, he asserts, "is not another step forward but a retreat to the classic approach. . . . The cold light of reason must be warmed by love."[21]

The final text of the *Catechism* shows some "warming" with its emphasis on freedom as "a force for growth and maturation in truth and goodness" (CCC 1731) and that "living a moral life bears witness to the dignity of the person" (CCC 1706). It also rearranges the material of the original draft to situate Christian morality in terms of an inclination toward "beatitude," claiming that our desire for happiness is a "natural" one (CCC 1718).

Our moral life, then, is seen as a positive response to the generous love of God that is deeply rooted in our nature. We are not foreigners to the kingdom; it is not far from our hearts. We do not "obey" a moral law so much as we "respond," naturally, to our most basic inclinations toward the good. This is what Cardinal Ratzinger would call "journeying with the Lord." It is what Jesus did and it is no less our calling as well.

For Further Reading

It cannot be stressed enough that the whole field of moral theology is undergoing some significant shifts. This period of transition can seem confusing and frustrating to the reader in search of clarity. However, it is possible to sift through the seemingly endless stream of contradictions and find some certainty. Though it can be somewhat esoteric and heavily philosophical at times, *Veritatis Splendor* is an excellent way to begin assessing the Church's moral "environment today." John Paul II has addressed some rather difficult issues in a succinct and direct manner. Along with this encyclical, reading *Gaudium et Spes* is a good way of situating the current direction we are taking in moral theology.

With that introduction, the interested reader should look to the history of moral theology as a way of "demystifying" our moral tradition. Although we would like to think of our history of morality as being a direct reflection of God's will, we know it has not been without its flaws. John Mahoney, in *The Making of Moral Theology* (Oxford: Clarendon Press, 1990) and Wayne Meeks, *The Origins of Christian Morality: The First Two Centuries* (New Haven: Yale University Press, 1993) offer two solidly written texts on how moral systems get formed.

There are many fine text-book summaries of Catholic moral theology that deserve attention. Three of the best include Richard Gula, *Reason Informed by Faith* (New York: Paulist Press, 1989); Timothy O'Connell, *Principles for a Catholic Morality*, revised edition (San Francisco: Harper and Row, 1990); Germain Grisez and Russell Shaw, *Fulfillment in Christ: A Summary of Christian Moral Principles* (Notre Dame: University of Notre Dame Press, 1991). I have also found George V. Lobo, *Guide to Christian Living: A New Compendium of Moral Theology* (Westminster Md.: Christian Classics, 1989) to be helpful in its organization and approachable rhetoric. And finally, Robin Gill, *A Textbook of Christian Ethics* (Edinburgh: T. & T. Clark Limited, 1989) is a wonderful resource for primary sources grouped together with classic and contemporary commentary.

No study of the Catholic moral tradition would be complete without the work of Bernard Haring. He is, quite simply, one of the most significant voices of this century in helping the Church rearticulate a morality that speaks to this modern age. His call for compassion, pastoral sensitivity, and tolerance is clearly evident in this final version of the catechism. His three-volume work *Free and Faithful in Christ* (Middlegreen: St. Paul Publications, 1979) is a comprehensive and challenging overview of Catholic/Christian morality that helped the Church begin to think more about its moral tradition in terms of responsible love rather than blind obedience.

Other contemporary authors who have made enormous contributions to the discussion of "revising" moral theology include Josef Fuchs, *Christian Ethics in a Secular Arena* (Washington, D.C.: Georgetown University Press, 1984); Charles Curran and Richard McCormick for their series *Readings in Moral Theology*, six Volumes (New York: Pueblo) published between 1980–1988 on a variety of topics. Lisa Sowle Cahill, *Between the Sexes: Foundations for a Christian Ethics of Sexuality* (Philadelphia: Fortress Press, 1985) offers a solid methodology for evaluating human actions; Vincent Genovesi, S.J., *In Pursuit of Love: Catholic Morality and Human Sexuality* (Collegeville, Minn.: Michael Glazier imprint, The Liturgical Press, 1987) includes a beautiful essay on "The Meaning and Spirit of Christian Living" that will help some readers to understand why a legalistic approach no longer speaks to the modern understanding of faith and morality.

Notes for Chapter 6

1. *Trenti Giorni* 11 (1992) 28–29.

2. Ibid.

3. All citations from *Gaudium et Spes* are taken from *Vatican Council II: The Conciliar and Post Conciliar Documents*, Austin Flannery, ed. (Collegeville, Minn.: The Liturgical Press, 1984).

4. Cf. *Gaudium et Spes*, 12. Richard Gula reminds us that human life is a reflection of God. This must serve as the beginning of any theological reflection. But it can also serve anthropologically because we believe that humanity was made in God's image; therefore, "it cannot be understood apart from God." See *Reason Informed by Faith* (New York: Paulist Press, 1989) 64–66. Gula carries the discussion one step further by saying that God is triune and that the relationship of the Trinity has a direct bearing on the relational nature of human existence.

5. Cf. *Gaudium et Spes*, 13. See also Bernard Haring, *Free and Faithful in Christ*, 3 vols. (New York: Crossroad, 1984); Haring has written extensively on this theme. Josef Fuchs, S.J., says that "Sin is the utterly destructive affirmation of self," a definition that highlights the relationship of sin to freedom. Fuchs insists that sin changes the sinner, not God. See his article "Sin and Conversion" in *Introduction to Christian Ethics: A Reader*. Ronald P. Hamel and Kenneth R. Himes, O.F.M., eds. (New York and New Jersey: Paulist Press, 1990) 206–216. In the same book see "Missing the Mark" by Bruce Vawter (199–205), in which sin is explored from an etymological perspective. The author suggests that maybe the reason we have lost a sense of sin is that we no longer know how to define it.

6. Cf. *Gaudium et Spes*, 14. See also *Veritatis Splendor*, 42–53 in which John Paul II makes a strong argument for the exalted nature of humanity.

7. Timothy O'Connell. *Principles for a Catholic Morality*, revised ed. (San Francisco: Harper and Row, 1990) 103–118.

8. Cf. *Gaudium et Spes*, 29.

9. Cf. *Gaudium et Spes*, 30.

10. Formulating a definition of moral norms can be somewhat tricky, but there is much that has been written on their "function." See *Veritatis Splendor*, 95–97; Gula, 283 ff.; Germain Grisez and Russell Shaw, *Fulfillment in Christ* (Notre Dame: University of Notre Dame Press, 1991) 111 ff. For an interesting insight from Hans Urs von Balthasar, see his essay "Nine Propositions on Christian Ethics," in which he sees the concrete existence of Christ as the norm that surpasses all others systems of ethical norms because the "synthesis of the Father's entire will that is achieved in the Person of Christ is eschatological and unsurpassable." Joseph Ratzinger, Heinz Schurmann, Hans Urs von Balthasar, *Principle of Christian Morality* (San Francisco: Ignatius Press, 1986) 82–83.

11. For a very helpful treatment of this complex issue, see John Mahoney, *The Making of Moral Theology* (Oxford: Clarendon Press, 1987) 72–115. Mahoney says that "[Thomas Aquinas] was of the view that the primary principles of the law of man's nature are known to all men, whereas when one begins to become more specific in drawing conclusions from such first principles, difficulty can arise. . . ." (105).

12. See Grisez and Shaw, *Fulfillment in Christ*. Chapter 10, entitled "From Modes of Responsibility to Moral Norms," addresses the care that must be taken in moving from the general to the specific, while strongly asserting that specific moral norms are possible to formulate and necessary for our moral well being.

13. Even though this shift may not be readily apparent, Richard Gula believes it is quietly changing the way we formulate moral norms. See *Reason Informed by Faith*, 30–39.

14. See Gula, 231–246 and Grisez and Shaw, 44–48.

15. See also CCC 1868, 1869.

16. *Commonweal* March 12, 1993, 10.

17. Cunningham says, "It does not strike me as impossible to say definite things about what we believe as Christians while, at the same time, giving some sense that we struggle to articulate the deep mystery of our faith, its paradoxical nature, and the challenges of a pluralistic world" *Commonweal* (12). John Mahoney says that one response to making moral distinctions is to "accept some distinctions as satisfying or helpful at least for the time being, while keeping an open mind to the possibility of their being further refined or eventually superseded." See his article "The Challenge of Moral Distinctions" in *Theological Studies* 53 (1992) 664.

18. "The Moral Vision of the Catechism" in *The Universal Catechism Reader: Reflections and Responses*, T. Reese, ed. (San Francisco: Harper, 1990) 137.

19. See Spohn's article "Magisterium and Morality: Notes on Moral Theology" in *Theological Studies* 54 (1993) 95–96.

20. "The New Catechism: Good News or Bad News?" *National Jesuit News*, March 1993.

21. Ibid.

CHAPTER 7

Christian Prayer

Francis Kelly Nemeck, O.M.I., and Marie Theresa Coombs, Hermit

The mystery of Christian prayer is the subject of the fourth and final part of the *Catechism of the Catholic Church*. Having treated the Creed in Part One, the sacraments in Part Two, ethical-moral issues in Part Three, the *Catechism* concludes in Part Four with prayer in the life of the Christian. This treatise is divided into two sections. Section One, "Prayer in the Christian Life," comprises three main headings: "The Revelation of Prayer," "The Tradition of Prayer," and "The Life of Prayer." Section Two presents an exposition of the Lord's Prayer.

Our intent in this chapter is fourfold. First, we highlight the *Catechism*'s general approach to prayer. Second, we offer some preliminary observations regarding Part Four as a whole. Third, we supplement the content of the *Catechism* with respect to three issues: (1) prayer in relation to the universal call to holiness, (2) prayer in twentieth-century North America, and (3) progress in prayer. Finally, we examine the Our Father not only as a prayer but also as a defining statement of the Christian covenant and as a basic method in praying.

THE CATECHISM'S APPROACH TO PRAYER

The opening paragraph of Part Four describes prayer in broad terms as a "vital and personal relationship with the living and true God" (CCC 2558). In an ecumenical gesture, the *Catechism* states that all religions bear witness to humanity's essential search for God (CCC 2566). It affirms a universal call to prayer, noting that the virtue of prayer is lived by many people in all religions (CCC 2569).

In a specifically Christian context, the *Catechism* looks at prayer from a Trinitarian perspective: "In the New Covenant, prayer is the living relationship of the children of God with their Father who is good beyond measure, with his Son Jesus Christ and with the Holy Spirit'' (CCC 2565). Then, accentuating the Christocentric nature of prayer, the text adds: ''Prayer is *Christian* insofar as it is a communion with Christ and extends throughout the Church, which is his Body. Its dimensions are those of Christ's love'' (CCC 2565).

In a positive light, the *Catechism* states that it is the whole person who prays (CCC 2562); that the sources of prayer include the Word of God, the liturgy, and the theological virtues (CCC 2652-2658); that prayer requires discernment (CCC 2663); that prayer draws life from the realities of creation (CCC 2569); that while we may designate specific times and places for prayer, communion with God ought to animate our lives at every moment (CCC 2697); that prayer is both a gift of grace and a determined response on our part (CCC 2725). The *Catechism's* attempt to be holistic regarding prayer comes out in this pithy sentence: ''We pray as we live, because we live as we pray'' (CCC 2725).

Despite those positive statements in the catechism, the anthropology underlying Part Four is mainly that of humanity separated from God and in need of salvation through rescuing by God. The *Catechism's* view of the world is primarily that of a hostile environment which tends to draw us away from God (CCC 2727) rather than a favorable support that nurtures us on our spiritual journey. Accordingly, the *Catechism* accentuates prayer more as a means of salvation — an expression of our effort to somehow reconnect with God — than as our loving response to the Trinity indwelling us. In this vein, the catechism describes prayer as a struggle ''against ourselves and against the wiles of the tempter'' who contrives to lure us away from prayer (CCC 2725). Quoting St. Alphonsus Liguori, Part Four states that ''those who pray are certainly saved; those who do not pray are certainly damned'' (CCC 2744).

PRELIMINARY OBSERVATIONS

The inclusion of a whole discourse on prayer bespeaks the importance that the *Catechism* gives to the subject in relation to Christian living. This recognition of prayer as a value on a par with the Creed, the sacraments, and ethical-moral conduct is perhaps the prime contribution of the *Catechism* to catechesis on prayer.

Prayer is at the core of Christian life for many reasons. In prayer we commune consciously and lovingly with Father, Son, and Spirit. In prayer we acquiesce to the divinizing and purifying influence of the Trinity dwelling in us. In prayer we cooperate with the transformative and purgative activity of God within us and all around us. Because loving intimacy is of the very essence of Christian prayer, we need not approach praying in an attitude of fear or burdensome duty. Rather, God invites us to pray in a stance of joyful trust in God's unconditional love.

As we survey the Table of Contents for the *Catechism*'s Part Four, we notice a logical sequence in the presentation of the material. However, when we enter a given chapter or article, we are inundated with a mass of information that in many instances is not coherently linked. Part Four is a smorgasbord of ideas about prayer, few of which are developed. Often, the *Catechism* presents these ideas in anthology form; that is, it lists a series of quotations predominantly from Scripture and Christian antiquity, with little explanation and virtually no contextualization.

With respect to biblical quotations, the *Catechism* chooses most of them appropriately. In some places, however, the scriptural references are so plentiful that they tend more to interrupt the flow of thought than to add insight. In a few places, the biblical citations seem forced.

The *Catechism*'s two sections on Mary (CCC 2617-2619 and 2673-2679) would have been greatly enhanced by a development of the spirituality that underlies the Lucan references to her prayer: Luke 1:38 (the "Fiat"); 1:46-55 (the "Magnificat"); 2:19 (at the birth of Jesus); 2:51 (in relation to the hidden life at Nazareth).[1]

With regard to the ancient Christian writers, we find twenty-three references in Part Four to Greek Fathers[2] and thirty-two references to Latin Fathers.[3] Yet, despite so many allusions to the first eight centuries of Christianity, the *Catechism* overlooks or omits some persons within that period who made outstanding contributions on the subject of prayer.[4]

From the eighth century to the present, the catechism refers explicitly to only six men: Guido the Carthusian († 1136) — CCC 2654; Thomas Aquinas († 1243) — CCC 2763; Ignatius of Loyola († 1556) — CCC 2715; John of the Cross († 1591) — CCC 2690, 2717; Alphonsus Liguori († 1787) — CCC 2744; and John Vianney († 1859) — CCC 2658.[5] Apart from its biblical references to Mary (CCC 2617-2619, 2673-2679), the catechism quotes just two women in all of Part Four: Teresa of Jesus

(† 1582) — CCC 2704, 2709, and Thérèse of the Child Jesus († 1897) — CCC 2558.[6]

Looking closely at the non-biblical authors cited, we notice that the composers of Part Four are clearly selective. With few exceptions, they limit their sources to Christian antiquity (i.e. to the first eight centuries of the Christian Era). Even within that period, there are omissions of certain writers and neglect of pivotal texts on prayer by authors cited. Beyond that period, the *Catechism* virtually reduces thirteen centuries of historical development of catechesis on prayer to this statement:

> In the living tradition of prayer, each Church proposes to its faithful, according to its historic, social and cultural context, a language for prayer: words, melodies, gestures, iconography (CCC 2663).

As for the few authors cited after the eighth century, the *Catechism* fails to include some of their most pertinent passages on prayer. This is the case, for example, with St. Ignatius of Loyola, St. Teresa of Jesus, and St. John of the Cross.

The sources for Part Four raise several questions: Did those who composed the *Catechism* not see any significant evolution in the catechesis of prayer after the first eight centuries? Would not the inclusion of teaching on prayer by more women have broadened the text's vision and enhanced its depth for all Catholics? While there are references to nine persons between the twelfth and the nineteenth centuries, how do we account for the complete lack of reference to development in the catechesis of prayer in the twentieth century?

A specific area of concern with respect to the *Catechism* is its analysis of prayer in terms of "meditation" (CCC 2705-2708) and "mental prayer" (CCC 2709-2719). The text's description of the distinction between these two forms of prayer is ambiguous, if not misleading. In effect, Part Four seems to equate mental prayer with meditation. In so doing, the catechism fails to recognize the development of mental prayer into what certain Catholic traditions have come to name "contemplation" — the wordless, imageless, direct, loving communion between God and the human person.[7]

Inadequate distinction between meditative forms of prayer and contemplation, strictly speaking, has repercussions in the article "The Struggle of Prayer" (CCC 2725-2751). While the advice offered in this section may be appropriate in the context of discursive prayer, that advice needs much nuancing and modification in the context of contemplation. For instance, the manner of handling dryness or dealing with distractions differs radically in meditation and contemplation.[8]

In general, the choice of language and the underlying mentality of Part Four come from another time and culture. Moreover, that outlook, combined with the *Catechism*'s basic anthropology and world view, tends to narrow and to confine its presentation on prayer. These conditions limit the usefulness of the text for catechists today in North America. In order to use Part Four in teaching, the catechist will have to re-think, re-contextualize, re-inculturate, re-formulate, and re-present virtually all of the *Catechism*'s content on prayer.

On the whole, unless the readers of the *Catechism* already possess considerable experience in praying, coupled with a reasonably well-developed theological framework in which to appraise the diverse modes and expressions of prayer, they will probably end up more befuddled than catechized by Part Four. Yet, those who do have both sufficient experience in praying and an adequate theological framework will find the *Catechism* woefully deficient. Sad to say, the masses of Catholics of all ages who are yearning for in-depth catechizing in prayer will not find it in this *Catechism*. While some insightful and inspiring passages exist among the 307 paragraphs that make up Part Four, these will not satisfy the profound hungering and thirsting of contemporary Christians for guidance in prayer.

THE CATECHISM'S PART FOUR, SECTION ONE: "PRAYER IN THE CHRISTIAN LIFE"

The lack of contextualization, especially in Section One (CCC 2558-2758), is a significant drawback in the use of the *Catechism*. To help readers situate its teaching in a broader perspective on prayer, we offer some reflections on three dimensions of this mystery: (1) the relationship of prayer to the universal call to holiness, (2) prayer in twentieth-century North America, (3) the developmental aspect of personal prayer.

Prayer and the Universal Call to Holiness

The first chapter of Part Four begins with the subtitle "The Universal Call to Prayer." Yet, the *Catechism* does not situate that calling within the more fundamental call of all the People of God to holiness.

Among the sixteen documents of Vatican II, one of the most seminal is *Lumen Gentium*, the Dogmatic Constitution on the Church. At the heart of that proclamation is Chapter V: "The Call of the Whole Church to Holiness." The gist of that chapter is expressed thus:

> The Lord Jesus . . . preached holiness of life to each and every one of his disciples, regardless of his/her situation: "You therefore are to be perfect, even as your heavenly Father is perfect" (Matt 5:48) — CCC 40.

The universal call to holiness means not only that the People of God as a whole is called to holiness, but also that each and every person is destined to become holy.[9]

In its biblical sense, holiness denotes the mysterious inner life of God. It refers to the intimacy that exists among the persons of the Trinity. Thus, to be called to holiness is to be destined to participate in the inner life and relatedness of Father, Son, and Spirit.

Through the centuries, official Church documents and various Christian writers have used a variety of terms to express something of that participation: "divinization," "deification," "sanctification," "spiritualization," "transformation." Although each of those words possesses its own nuance, they all converge on the same mystery: God enabling us to commune ever more deeply in the Trinity's own life. By being thus transformed in God by God, we move toward the fullness of our personhood. This process has already begun in us by virtue of the divine indwelling. Indeed, it begins when we begin.

Our initiation into the process of participation in God is celebrated in baptism and confirmation. Our continued growth in that process is symbolized and nurtured in the Eucharist. Throughout our spiritual journey, daily prayer is a privileged context of conscious loving communion with God indwelling us. Prayer is thus a touchstone and a matrix of God's calling us to holiness, to divine intimacy, to self-actualization.

We undergo God's transformation of us twenty-four hours a day, seven days a week. Yet, we are not always aware of that divine presence and activity. Prayer, then, is a privileged moment each day when we put aside everything else in order to consciously abide with God in mystery. Prayer is a deliberate leaving our usual works and concerns for a time in order to celebrate the life and the love that animate them. St. Teresa of Jesus captures the gist of this experience in describing what she understands by mental prayer:

> Mental prayer is nothing else than a friend-to-Friend exchange and
> a frequent solitary communion with the One whom we know loves
> us.[10]

Or as she puts it in slightly different terms a little later in her autobiography:

> You need do no more than remain there with God . . . beholding
> the One who is beholding you.[11]

As important as is the Creed (Part One of the *Catechism*), it is not
enough that we believe certain truths related to the divine indwelling.
As significant as are the sacraments (Part Two) it is not enough to
celebrate in symbol and in mystery certain facets of the divine indwelling. As necessary as is a well-formed conscience (Part Three), it is not
enough to have good moral attitudes and conduct flowing from the
divine indwelling. In order to become holy as God is holy, we must
also in prayer consciously and lovingly commune with Father, Son,
and Spirit indwelling us.

PRAYER IN TWENTIETH-CENTURY NORTH AMERICA

The first chapter of Part Four acknowledges the interrelatedness of
prayer and history:

> Prayer is bound up with human history, for it is the relationship
> with God in historical events (CCC 2568).

However, the *Catechism*'s attempt at a historical survey of the understanding and the practice of prayer is limited to four areas: (1) consideration of prayer in the lives of Abraham, Moses, David, and Elijah
(CCC 2570-2584); (2) reference to the psalms as the prayer of the assembly (CCC 2585-2589); (3) discussion of the prayer of Jesus and Mary
(CCC 2598-2619); and (4) mention of specific forms of prayer — blessing, adoration, petition, intercession, thanksgiving, and praise — in
the Age of the Church (CCC 2623-2643).

Regarding prayer in the Age of the Church, the reader of Part Four
is apt to get the impression that the Christian understanding of prayer,
as well as the experience of praying, has remained practically un-
changed since the time of Jesus. Yet, both the word "prayer" and the
practice of praying have a long and complex evolution. Although an

unfolding of that development is beyond the scope of this chapter, catechists could greatly benefit from knowledge of the evolving history of prayer.[12] In this section, we focus on historical developments regarding prayer in twentieth-century North America for two principal reasons: (1) This continent is the context of catechesis for most readers of this chapter; and (2) the *Catechism* makes no reference to this period.

In the twentieth century, the turning point for Catholics in their theology, spiritual life, and practice of prayer is the Second Vatican Council (1962-1965). Thus, for all practical purposes, we can consider discourse on prayer and expression of prayer in the daily lives of Catholics in terms of "before" and "after" Vatican II.[13]

The Second Vatican Council did not produce a document specifically on prayer. Nonetheless, its liturgical renewal, with insistence on the vernacular and on the inculturation of rites of worship, opened up for the average person in the pews vast new horizons for prayer. Quickly following the Council came, in North America, the charismatic revival, the formation of base ecclesial communities, and the establishment of small prayer groups.[14] These movements caught on like wild fire. They afforded unlimited varieties of spontaneous and shared prayer to vast numbers of people who had assumed that the only ways to pray were memorized or repetitious formulas such as rosaries, litanies, and novenas.

The House of Prayer movement in North America — ignited in the late 1960s and early 1970s — continues to furnish vast numbers of people with actual places to go in order to nurture their prayer and to seek competent spiritual direction in prayer.[15] In relation to this point, Part Four has a section entitled "Suitable Places for Prayer" (CCC 2691, 2696). Conspicuous by its absence is any mention of houses of prayer, retreat centers, Christian ashrams, etc. The catechism's closest acknowledgement of these suitable milieus for prayer is its reference in CCC 2689 to "prayer groups" and "schools of prayer." Yet, even then, "concern for communion" nuances and conditions the value of these means of renewal. In North America alone, retreat centers, houses of prayer, and Christian ashrams currently number approximately seven hundred.

One characteristic of post-Vatican II theology is the increasing trend toward interdisciplinary studies, for example, theology and psychology, theology and feminism, theology and ecology, theology and aesthetics. Each area of interdisciplinary study has made a positive contribution to the theology and the practice of prayer. The dialogue between theology and psychology, for instance, has led to the study of how various prayer forms relate to different personality types.[16] The dialogue between theology and aesthetics, for example, is awakening a renewal of interest in prayer as dance, song, painting, sculpturing.[17]

Vatican II gave ecumenism an enormous boost. Consequently, many Catholics have enriched their understanding of prayer with the insights of authors from other Christian traditions.[18] Dialogue between Christianity and world religions, especially Oriental mysticisms, has also contributed significantly to developments in transcendental meditation and contemplative prayer.[19]

In summary, out of a history spanning four millenniums, the twentieth century, with Vatican II as the focal event for Catholics, has been especially fertile soil for the practice and the understanding of prayer. In North America, salient features of this period include:

- Rekindling of interest in and adaptation of fourth-, fifth-, and sixth-century desert spirituality. Contemporary expressions of Centering Prayer, Christian Meditation, the Jesus Prayer, and the Prayer of the Heart typify this development.[20]

- Renewed popular interest in Ignatian approaches to prayer. Exemplifying this trend is the revival, especially among the laity, of thirty-day retreats and the 19th Annotation, as well as of related prayer forms such as the Prayer of Christ's Memories, the Prayer of Personal Reminiscence, Ignatian Contemplation and methods of Christian discernment.[21]

- Renewed popular interest in Carmelite approaches to prayer. Widespread participation in courses, institutes, and retreats inspired by the spirituality of St. Teresa of Jesus and St. John of the Cross witness to this current.[22]

- Integration of prayer and social justice, of prayer and apostolic community, of prayer and the preferential option for the poor.[23]

- Increasing use of scripturally based prayer, especially the ''Prayer of the Church'' (i.e., the Liturgy of the Hours) by more of the People of God, notably the laity.[24]

- Many forms and occasions of ecumenical prayer, for example, the Taizé Prayer for Unity and Prayer for Church Unity Week.[25]

- Adaptation of prayer to culture, a theme frequently promoted by Pope John Paul II, and the creative searching for myths, symbols, and rituals that speak both out of and to contemporary human experience. This searching includes new appreciation for native (i.e., aboriginal) North American prayer practices as well as renewed sensitivity to feminine and masculine archetypes.[26]

- Prayer forms that honor creation, for example, prayer as movement and art, prayer as imagination, prayer in relation to ecology, posture and breathing as aspects of prayer, anointing and healing prayer celebrations.[27]
- Growth of associations and programs for the training and the ongoing formation of spiritual directors from all walks of life and diverse ecclesial affiliations.[28]
- Celebrations of public liturgy, especially the Eucharist, that are becoming more inculturated, participative, and gender inclusive.
- Development of prayer and inner healing practices in relation to 12-Step programs for the addicted, the codependent, and the victims of abuse.[29]
- Proliferation of books, periodicals, and tapes on prayer and related spirituality, as well as courses, institutes, and other programs of formation in prayer.[30]
- Perhaps above all, a clearly recognizable thirsting and hungering among people generally for prayer and for God.

PROGRESS IN PRAYER

The *Catechism's* Part Four contains no meaningful discussion on progress in prayer. Not only does it fail to mention the considerable evolution in the understanding and practice of prayer over the centuries, but the catechism does not even acknowledge progress in the prayer life of individual Christians. That lack, coupled with Part Four's ambiguous presentation of the distinctions between various forms of prayer (CCC 2705-2719), can prove confusing and misleading to readers.

Prayer is at the heart of our response to God's calling us to holiness. In prayer, we commune with God as the Spirit transforms us and draws us ever deeper into divine intimacy. Yet, most of us do not start off in prayer consciously abiding in the simplicity of loving communion with God. The Spirit only gradually draws us into greater affective relatedness. We grow slowly into communion with the One who first loves us. Thus, there is progression in prayer.

Spiritual authors have diverse ways of describing the development of personal prayer. We synthesize four approaches: that of (1) St. Ignatius of Loyola, (2) St. John of the Cross, (3) St. Teresa of Jesus, and (4) that of a contemporary model.

Progress in Prayer
According to St. Ignatius of Loyola

The Ignatian approach to prayer is very rich. Entire books have been written about it.[31] Here, we focus on one point: the difference between Ignatian meditation and Ignatian contemplation.

Meditation in the context of the Ignatian Exercises is an arduous and detailed delving into a given mystery of salvation, into a specific passage from Scripture or from a spiritual author, or into the meaning of some virtue that the person meditating needs to apply to his/her life. Most of the meditation period is taken up with thinking, analyzing, pondering, deliberating, reflecting, examining, evaluating, reviewing, etc. The purpose of all this activity is to lead the person meditating to an explicit act of love toward God, to a conversion of attitude and behavior, or to a specific resolution in view of improving one's life.

Contemplation in the context of the Ignatian Exercises is less toilsome and more intentionally receptive than meditation. When I meditate on, for instance, a Gospel passage, I work it over; whereas when I contemplate a Gospel passage, I tend to let it work me over. Ignatian contemplation accentuates entering into a Gospel scene and becoming a participant, for example, by being one of the guests enjoying new wine at the wedding feast of Cana, by sitting on the mountainside listening to the Beatitudes, by standing near the cross with Mary and John as they experience the passion of Jesus. Ignatian contemplation uses a very active imagination that engages the senses. In this way, the person contemplating tries to touch, to hear, to smell, to see, to taste something of what might have transpired had s/he been present at the original scene. The purpose of this participation is to deepen loving affinity with the person of Jesus and with his mission.

According to this Ignatian approach, a key dimension of progression in prayer is the transition from greater activity on the part of the one praying (Ignatian meditation) to more loving receptivity (Ignatian contemplation). In the latter, God's activity is more directly transformative than our activity could ever be.

Progress in Prayer
According to St. John of the Cross

John has many insightful descriptions of prayer.[32] All of them, however, boil down to this: To pray means ultimately to remain loving one's

Beloved, the lover being transformed in the Beloved. This experience of prayer presupposes two truths: (1) that the one praying is aware that God has first loved him/her uniquely and personally with an everlasting love, and (2) that the one praying cooperates most intensely with God by letting God's love elicit his/her love in return.

John understands prayer from basically two points of view: discursive prayer and contemplative prayer.

"Discursive" encompasses all forms of liturgical, communal, meditative, shared, oral prayer. This includes the Mass, the rosary, novenas, litanies, Ignatian contemplation, speaking in tongues, saying one's prayers, and the like. Two qualities are common to discursive forms of praying: (1) Although God remains the initiator and the enabler, I am — or in the case of the liturgy, the Church is — the principal agent in the act of praying. I am the one praying. I pray in such-and-such a manner. (2) There exists a medium of interchange between the person praying and God: voice, sight, touch, symbol, gesture, sacrament, concept, thought, action, language, image, etc. God and I commune in prayer through some means.

On the other hand, contemplative prayer according to John of the Cross is silent loving abandonment to God dwelling within oneself and in all creation. In contemplation, God is the principal agent. God prays me. I am prayed. God prays me, however, without my going through the mediums characteristic of discursive prayer. In contemplation, God and I commune directly and immediately in my inmost being, without words, gestures, or images. In contemplation, I commune with all creation in and through God.

As modes of praying, discursive prayer and contemplation are not only basic but also successive. By virtue of its inner dynamics, discursive prayer tends toward and eventually gives way to contemplation. Although certain forms of liturgical prayer, especially the Eucharist, remain meaningful throughout life, the one praying grows to appreciate fewer words, less motion, and more silence, even at Mass. The transition can be relatively quick and clean-cut or it can extend over many years with a certain back-and-forth movement. In any case, God and God alone effects the transition, doing so in a manner that respects all the particulars of an individual's existence. This overall direction toward more intentional quiet and more explicit loving receptivity in prayer is not just the prerogative of a few people. In virtue of the universal call to holiness, it is the spiritual direction of each and every person.

Progress in prayer according to St. John of the Cross means, therefore, making the transition from "me praying to God" to "God praying me, I letting it be done." The more I am receptive to the divine intimacy within me and the divine activity all around me, the more efficaciously the Spirit is transforming me in God and recapitulating all things in Christ. Essentially, this is the "Fiat" of Mary who not only did God's will but also acquiesced to God's will being done in and through her.

Progress in Prayer
According to St. Teresa of Jesus

Perhaps the most familiar explanation of progress in prayer according to Teresa of Jesus pertains to what she calls "mental prayer" and to her development of that theme in chapters 8 to 23 of her autobiography. Teresa goes into more depth and detail regarding prayer in other works.[33] Yet, the presentation in her *Life* establishes an excellent foundation for catechetical instruction.[34]

Rather than insist on the words "meditation" and "contemplation," which admitted of various understandings, Teresa used the phrase "mental prayer." Teresa describes mental prayer basically as a solitary friend-to-Friend intimacy with God dwelling within her. Thus, the word "mental" for Teresa does not denote "cerebral" or "heady," but rather "inmost." Mental prayer, then, is a mode of prayer emanating from the deepest recesses of the human person.

According to Teresa, that affective communing evolves. She illustrates its development through the image of watering a garden. The first way of watering is by means of a well and a bucket. Here, the gardener exerts enormous energy: lowering the bucket, drawing it up, carrying it over to the plant, pouring it out, then repeating the action for each shrub and tree. The second way of watering the garden is by means of a hand pump and something like a hose. This is less arduous, but it still requires considerable work. The third way is by irrigation, which is less tedious still and more efficacious. The fourth way of watering the garden is simply to sit on the porch and let the rain soak everything.

Teresa's description of the first watering is comparable to Ignatian meditation. The second is suggestive of Ignatian contemplation. The third way approximates what St. John of the Cross calls the beginning of contemplation (according to his understanding of the term "contemplation" as distinct from Ignatius). The fourth watering is comparable to what John understands as full-blown contemplation. In this last way of praying, we are completely receptive and at rest while God does the work.

In her analogy of watering to describe progress in prayer, Teresa clearly accentuates the movement away from much activity on the part of the person praying toward an ever-increasing loving receptiveness to God's activity.

Progress in Prayer: A Contemporary Model

Basing ourselves primarily on the three above approaches and on certain insights of Pierre Teilhard de Chardin, we now outline our own description of the prayer development that most people undergo in the process of their transformation in God, by God.[35]

In his Second Letter to the Corinthians, St. Paul offers this insight into the transformative process:

> As the outer person is falling into decay, the inner person is being renewed day by day (2 Cor 4:16).

The process of exterior disintegration and interior renewal is like two parallel yet interrelated lines simultaneously moving forward until finally they coincide in our personal death/resurrection. At that ultimate threshold, the outer person turns entirely to dust and the inner person reaches consummate transformation in God. Both movements span our entire lifetime, from the womb to the tomb. The line of the decaying outer person suggests the intensifying dark night of the soul. The line of inner renewal implies evolving personal transformation in God, by God.

Integral to this lifelong process of aging and maturing is a twofold rhythm: *immersion* in creation for Christ and *emergence* through creation with Christ. These are but two phases of a single movement: like breathing in and breathing out; like the arsis and thesis of a musical measure.

Although immersion and emergence occur simultaneously throughout life, at different periods of our development we are more conscious of one or the other. Early in life, we tend to focus principally on immersion. In later life, the realization of emergence becomes more explicit.

From the perspective of experiential awareness, then, immersion and emergence can designate two successive stages of the spiritual journey. As we progress in prayer throughout each stage, these three factors undergo change: (1) our perception of God, (2) our mode of praying, and (3) our experience of prayer.

Immersion in creation for Christ represents that stage of the spiritual journey in which we must increase so that Christ can increase in us and all around us. Immersion accentuates the *kataphatic* dimension of encounter with God, that is, the more observable or light-imbued aspect of spiritual progress. We develop our talents. We take advantage of the opportunities that come our way. We build up as rich a personhood and as productive a life as circumstances permit. In imitation of the Word Incarnate, we immerse ourselves in creation, and there, mingling with created things, take hold of and disengage from them all that they contain of life eternal.

For most of us, this immersion is so connatural that we rarely advert to it as a stage of spiritual development. For many of us, immersion as a stage coincides with the years from birth to midlife.

Optimally, early immersion stretches across infancy, childhood, and the beginning of adolescence. Our typical perception of God at this time is God as Creator, God as Almighty — in street language, the great Fixer-upper in the sky. Our typical modes of praying during this stage include the recitation of prayers composed by others (e.g., the Hail Mary, the Apostle's Creed); more formal prayers (e.g., the rosary, litanies); spontaneous prayers (e.g., night prayers, grace before meals). Our typical experience of prayer during early immersion is that prayer is fun. Generally, praying at this time is enjoyable. It makes us feel good. It gives positive strokes.

As we progress beyond the early phases of immersion in creation, we eventually reach a critical threshold wherein we become "spiritual adults." We desire to foster a personal relationship with Jesus. We consciously and willingly commit ourselves to Christ. Optimally, immersion as an interior threshold corresponds to the psychological and spiritual awakenings of late adolescence and early adulthood.

Our typical perception of God during this more advanced phase of immersion is that of Friend, someone with whom we are at ease and can converse readily. Among our typical modes of praying at this time, meditation is prominent. That meditation does not, however, remain static. In the course of our immersion, it evolves into a simplified, affective form of discursive prayer. At least initially, our typical experience in meditating is that of meaningfulness. Meditation makes sense; it is personally significant. Little by little, however, that sense of meaningfulness wanes and a certain dutifulness begins to dominate — "I ought to or should continue meditating, even if I find it increasingly difficult." For many people, prayer that had begun as meaningful and was continued as dutiful eventually reaches an alarming dead end. On a feeling level, they experience their prayer as useless and even as drudgery. Needless to say, these sentiments cause intense pain and profound anxiety in the person trying to seek lovingly a God who seems ever more distant. Many people abandon prayer altogether in this context — especially extended solitary prayer.

Paradoxically, this enigmatic shifting and apparent regression may be signs of progress in prayer. It is difficult to imagine that experiencing prayer as useless, meaningless, or drudgery can actually indicate growth in intimacy with God. Yet, as light casts a shadow, so deepening communion with God causes aridity, spiritual anxiety, and an inability to pray as before.[36] This is what we mean: If we are true to life and to grace, we cannot continue indefinitely in the direction of full human development of our energies and talents. Gradually, and as a result of our immersion in creation for Christ, we become aware of a new direction forming within us. This movement grows steadily more dominant and eventually changes our previous impulse toward building up self. This new direction expresses itself mysteriously as a predilection for detachment: I must decrease so that Christ may further increase both within me and around me (see John 3:30).

The inevitable experience of human life is that we have hardly arrived at the zenith of our accomplishments when we are ready to leave them and to move on. Having taken our fill of the world and of ourselves, we discover within us an intense need to die to self and to leave all self-interests behind. Moreover, for the person faithful to life and to grace, this predilection for detachment is not the result of failure or despair. Rather it is the normal outcome of effort and success.

Thus begins the next stage of our formation in Christ Jesus: that of passing all the way through creation (or of emergence) with him. This new direction accentuates the *apophatic*, that is, the more mysterious or dark aspect of our encounter with God's transforming and purifying love.

Optimally, the stage of emergence through creation with Christ encompasses midlife and beyond. Whether we have abandoned prayer or persevered in it, as we enter this stage our typical perception of God has progressed from Almighty and Friend to Beloved. God is drawing us irresistibly into increasing intimacy. Our typical mode of praying at this time is what St. John of the Cross calls the beginning of contemplation. Moreover, once the Spirit has led us into contemplation, the depths of loving receptivity into which God may draw us are limitless. Our typical experience of prayer, once we begin going with the flow of emergence, is that of prayer as a hunger — and ultimately as a need. We simply must have extended time in solitary prayer each day, just as we must have proper rest and nourishment. We need quality time alone with God, just as lovers need to spend time together.

To supplement the content of the *Catechism,* we have outlined above four models describing progress in personal prayer. Why is it important for readers of the *Catechism* to be acquainted with such models? Primarily for this reason: When people begin to pray, a need for guidance and direction emerges. Catechists will ordinarily be among those first called upon to address these pastoral issues.

THE CATECHISM'S PART FOUR, SECTION TWO: THE LORD'S PRAYER . . . OUR FATHER!

Most people think of the Our Father as *a prayer,* and indeed it is. The Lord's Prayer is recited during the celebration of the Eucharist. It introduces each decade of the rosary, and concludes certain hours of the Prayer of the Church. It is as a prayer that Section Two of Part Four takes up the Our Father, giving each of its seven phrases an anthology-like commentary (CCC 2759-2865). Yet, the Our Father remains much more than a prayer. It is also a basic statement of the Christian covenant and a concretely suggested procedure in praying.[37]

There are two presentations of the Our Father in the New Testament: Matthew 6:9-13 and Luke 11:1-4. Biblical scholars estimate that Luke's version is probably the oldest form lengthwise, while Matthew's version is probably the more original in terms of actual wording. That is, Luke may have changed certain words so that his predominantly Gentile readership could better comprehend the meaning of the prayer. Matthew, on the other hand, may have added a few phrases to the original formula so that his predominantly Jewish readership could better grasp the sense of the prayer. In any case, the *Didache* took Matthew's text, added the doxology, and prescribed that all Christians pray the Our Father daily.

Matthew incorporates the Lord's Prayer into Jesus' Sermon on the Mount, presumably given somewhere on the northern shores of the Sea of Galilee. Luke, on the other hand, situates the Lord's Prayer after Jesus's encounter with Martha and Mary in Bethany, presumably somewhere on or near the Mount of Olives. Historically and geographically, Luke is probably more accurate.

Luke's introduction to the Our Father (Luke 11:1-2) is significant:

> [Jesus] was praying in a certain place, and after he had finished, one of his disciples said to him, "Lord, teach us to pray, as John taught his disciples." He said to them, "When you pray, say . . ."

The actual scene may have been something like this: Several disciples were gathered, possibly sitting around a campfire, while Jesus was alone some distance way. They had the impression that he was praying, whatever prayer may have meant to them at the time. After a while, Jesus joined them. It was at this point that one of them, probably a former disciple of John the Baptist, spoke up.

In effect, the disciple is asking Jesus for two things: (1) a "word" to identify him specifically as a disciple of Jesus, and (2) a procedure in praying: how to pray.

AN IDENTIFYING "WORD"

At the time of Jesus, it was common for disciples of a master to identify themselves with some "word" — a kind of password unique to the group. Thus, in a sense, this disciple is saying: "John had given us his specific identifying word. So, Lord, what is yours?" Jesus took this opportunity to make one of the most startling and intimate revelations of the New Covenant: *Abba*. God is not only Father, *Abh*, but *Abba*. The word *Abba* was the most affectionate and intimate way that a child could address his/her father — something akin to "Daddy" or "Papa" in our culture.

In the Middle East, as far back as the third millennium before the Christian Era, we find examples of deities being called "Father." In the Hebrew Scriptures, over a dozen times God is addressed or referred to as *Abh*, Father. The sense of those texts is not so much procreator or ancestor but rather one who has chosen and saved his people, his dear children (see Isa 63:16; 64:7; Jer 3:4). The Talmud speaks of *abba* and *imma* as the first words of an infant: "Dada" and "Mama."

Yet, neither the Hebrew Scriptures nor Judaism ever dared refer to God as *Abba*.

Clearly, St. Paul considered our ability to call God *Abba* a unique privilege. According to Paul, only the Holy Spirit can enable us to recognize God as *Abba*:

> For you did not receive a spirit of slavery to fall back into fear, but you have received a spirit of adoption. When we cry "Abba! Father! it is the Spirit of God bearing witness with our spirit that we are children of God . . . (Rom 8:15).

Not only does Jesus call his Father *Abba*, but also the Holy Spirit indwelling us addresses the Father as *Abba*. The Spirit does this both for us and with us:

> And because you are children, God has sent the Spirit of his Son into our hearts, crying, Abba! Father! (Gal 4:6; see Rom 8:26-27).

In his cry to God from the cross, Jesus quotes Psalm 22:1 "Eloi, Eloi . . . My God, my God . . ." (Matt 27:47; Mark 15:34). However, on every other occasion in the Gospel when Jesus addresses God, he does so as Father. Among those instances, Mark preserves for us the *ipsissima vox Iesu* (i.e., the actual sound of the very word that Jesus used) in the wrenching moments of his agony in the garden:

> *Abba*, Father . . . remove this cup from me; yet, not what I will, but what you will (Mark 14:36).

One cannot exaggerate the importance of Jesus calling his Father *Abba*. Jesus could not have expressed the depth of intimacy between himself and his Father in a more tender and loving way. Nor can one exaggerate the significance of the fact that Jesus invites us, his followers, to address his Father and our Father by the same name — a name that expresses the fullness of God's love and intimacy, caring and compassion, tenderness and mercy for us. That is why we *"dare* to say": *Abba*, our Father.

The word *Abba* is also a window into mysteries such as the Trinity, the incarnation, the identity and the mission of Jesus, divine providence, the transformation of each and every one of us in God, by God.

Thus, when the unnamed disciple asked Jesus for a "word," he received a revelation that we are still trying to fathom, even after two thousand years.

HOW TO PRAY

In Luke 11:1, the disciple asked Jesus also how to pray: "Lord, teach us to pray."

The Lord responded not only with a formula — a prayer — but also with a method of praying — a concretely suggested procedure in addressing *Abba*, our Father. We say "concretely suggested procedure" because in revealing the framework common to all Christian praying, Jesus — *the* catechist par excellence — respected the mentality of his immediate audience. Had he not done so, the people whom he was catechizing would not have understood him. One characteristic of Semitic thought and language at the time was the dominance of concrete images and formulas in contradistinction to abstract concepts or schemas.

Viewing the Lord's Prayer as a concretely suggested procedure in praying, we perceive three basic elements: adoration, petition, and contrition. Statements of adoration include: "*Abba*, Father . . . Holy is your name." Statements of petition include "Give us today our daily bread." Statements of contrition include "Forgive us our trespasses."

What is adoration in essence? Adoration brings into explicit consciousness the reality of God to us. By adoration, we put ourselves in the presence of God, so to speak, beholding God as God. Father, Son, and Spirit are always present to us; indeed, abiding within us. Yet, we are not always conscious of that divine intimacy and indwelling. So, by adoration we — as reflecting, loving human beings — explicitly acknowledge that reality.

What is petition in essence? Petition is the conscious and affective positing of the truth of our total dependence upon our Father. In reality, we depend on God for absolutely everything: from our individual existence to the bread we eat and the water we drink. Yet, we are not always aware of that dependence. So, any petition — be it general or particular — acknowledges implicitly this all-embracing truth: I am a son or a daughter, utterly dependent upon my loving Father.

What is contrition in essence? Contrition is my response to the stark awareness of the actual relationship that exists between God and me: I am a sinner, and God is my loving *Abba*. "I fail to do what I want to do, and I find myself carrying out the very things I hate . . ." (Rom 7:15). There is a "law of sin" (Rom 7:23) that operates within me, causing an aspect of me to be alienated from God and from my deepest self. This dimension of my personhood is in rebellious opposition to

Truth, Goodness, and Love. Contrition means facing the antagonism between my self-centeredness and God. It is owning up to my infidelity and need for repentance. Christian contrition is the humble and sorrowful surrender of this rebelliousness to the inscrutable fidelity and tender mercy of *Abba*, my Father.

Thus, all prayer comprises these three elements: adoration (which includes also praise and thanksgiving), petition (which includes also intercession), and contrition (which includes also repentance).

According to Luke 11:1-4, Jesus taught his disciples to pray in distinct and successive acts: first, acts of adoration . . . then, acts of petition . . . and finally, acts of contrition. . . . This sequence of acts — first, placing oneself knowingly and affectively in the presence of God; then, acknowledging one's dependence on God, followed by an awareness of the relationship that exists between oneself and God — accords profoundly with the patterns of consciousness common to most people. Making specific acts of adoration, petition, and contrition is an effective and concrete way of expressing the most basic truth of human existence: God is more lovingly present to me than I am to myself, and before God I am a sinner who is totally dependent on my *Abba*'s love and forgiveness.

We can carry Luke's Our Father scene a step further. We may well wonder how Jesus would have responded if the disciple in Luke 11:1, after practicing for a considerable time the method he had received, could have asked: "Now, Lord, how should I pray?" That is, as the disciple advanced from beginner to proficient in prayer, in which direction would his prayer have evolved? In other words, what constitutes progress in prayer?

Progress in prayer is characterized by the gradual transformation of distinct and successive acts (adoration, petition, contrition) into the simplicity of loving abandonment. As our prayer matures, we become increasingly more disinclined toward a multiplicity of discursive acts and ever more inclined toward the wordless, imageless, loving receptivity of contemplation: beholding our *Abba* beholding us.

As such, contemplation is both one prayer form among many and the apex of all prayer. It is one expression of prayer because in the course of a day, a week, a month, a person's prayer-life will comprise many expressions and forms: liturgical, oral, communal, private, etc. It is also the apex of all prayer because inherent even to all modes of discursive prayer is an inner propensity toward loving surrender to God. In fact, the final human act of each person — in death — is none other than a simple act of loving abandonment: "Here I am, Lord; take me." "Amen! Come, Lord Jesus" (Rev 22:20). As each and every one is called to holiness, so each and every one is called — at least in death — to the simplicity of loving abandonment. That loving surrender is the quintessence of contemplation.

The *Catechism*, quoting Tertullian, designates the Lord's Prayer as "the summary of the whole gospel" (CCC 2761). According to the *Catechism*, it is a summary primarily in the sense of the specific content implied in its individual verses. In truth, the Our Father is so rich that catechists can present it not only as "a prayer" incorporating the core elements of the good news, but also as a method in praying and as a model to describe progress in prayer.

Notes for Chapter 7

1. See, for example: Leonardo Boff, *The Maternal Face of God* (San Francisco: Harper & Row, 1987) 107–121; Raymond E. Brown, *The Birth of the Messiah* (Garden City, N.Y.: Doubleday, 1977) 316–319, 346–365; Jules Lebreton S.J., *The Spiritual Teaching of the New Testament* (Westminster, Md.: Newman, 1960) 85–132.

2. Ignatius of Antioch, † 110 (one time); Origen of Alexandria, † 254 (three); Cyril of Jerusalem, † 358 (four); Basil of Cappadocia, † 379 (one); Gregory of Nazianzus, † 390 (three); Gregory of Nyssa, † 395 (one); John Chrysostom, † 407 (six), Evagrius Ponticus, † 398 (two); Isaac of Nineveh, 6th cent. (one); and John Damascene, † 730 (one).

3. Tertullian of Carthage, † 230 (six times); Cyprian of Carthage, † 258 (six); Ambrose of Milan, † 397 (five); Augustine of Hippo, † 430 (ten); John Cassian, † 450 (one); Peter Chrysologus, † 454 (three); and Benedict of Nursia, † 543 (one).

4. These include: Hilary of Poitiers, † 368; Pseudo-Dionysius, 3rd to 5th centuries; Gregory the Great, † 604.

5. Notable male authors on prayer since Christian antiquity who are not referred to in Part Four include: Anselm of Canterbury, † 1109; Hugh of St Victor, † 1141; William of St. Thierry, † 1148; Bernard of Clairvaux, † 1153; Bonaventure of Albano, † 1274; the Rhino-Flemish mystics (especially Meister Eckhart, † 1328; John Tauler, † 1361; Henry Suso, † 1366), the author of *The Cloud of Unknowing*, 14th century; Luis of Granada, † 1588; Francis Suarez, † 1617; Francis de Sales, † 1622; Pierre de Bérulle, † 1629; Augustine Baker, † 1641; Jean-Jacques Olier, † 1657; Jean-Pierre de Caussade, † 1751; Augustin Poulain, † 1919; Réginald Garrigou-Lagrange, † 1964; Romano Guardini, † 1968; Thomas Merton, † 1968; Karl Rahner, † 1984.

6. Noteworthy female teachers on prayer from the Middle Ages to the present who are not mentioned in Part Four include: Hildegard of Bingen, † 1179; Mechthild of Magdeburg, † 1294; Mechtild of Hackeborn, † 1298; Hadewijch, 13th century; Gertrude of Helfta, † 1302; Marguerite Porete, † 1310; Julian of Norwich, † 1420; Margery Kempe, † 1439; Margaret Mary Alacoque, † 1690; Elizabeth of the Trinity, † 1906; Edith Stein, † 1942.

7. See, for example: Francis Kelly Nemeck, O.M.I., and Marie Theresa Coombs, Hermit, *The Spiritual Journey: Critical Thresholds and Stages of Adult Spiritual Genesis* (Collegeville, Minn.: The Liturgical Press, 1987) 76–88, 114–124; James Finley, *The Awakening Call* (Notre Dame, Ind.: Ave Maria, 1984); Thomas Merton, O.C.S.O., *Contemplative Prayer* (Garden City, N.Y.: Image, 1971) 67–116; Thomas H. Green, S.J., *Opening to God* (Notre Dame, Ind.: Ave Maria, 1977) and *When the Well Runs Dry* (1979); Romano Guardini, *Prayer in Practice* (New York: Pantheon, 1957) 42–99, 134–156; Marie-Eugène, O.C.D., *I Want to See God* (Chicago: Fides, 1953) 49–63, 183–213, 234–249, 456–474.

8. See, for example: Francis Kelly Nemeck, O.M.I., and Marie Theresa Coombs, Hermit, *Contemplation* (Collegeville, Minn.: The Liturgical Press, 1982) 53–96; Alexandre Brou, S.J., *Ignatian Methods of Prayer* (Milwaukee: Bruce, 1949); Simon Tugwell, O.P. *Prayer in Practice* (Springfield, Ill.: Templegate, 1974); Marie-Eugène, O.C.D., *I Am a Daughter of the Church* (Chicago: Fides, 1955) 3–123; Antonio Royo, O.P., and Jordan Aumann, O.P., *The Theology of Christian Perfection* (Dubuque, Ia.: Priory Press, 1962) 499–561; Réginald Garrigou-Lagrange, O.P., *Christian Perfection and Contemplation* (St. Louis: B. Herder, 1937) 199–336; Edward Leen, C.S.Sp., *Progress through Mental Prayer* (New York: Sheed & Ward, 1935).

9. See Francis Kelly Nemeck, O.M.I., and Marie Theresa Coombs, Hermit, *Called by God: A Theology of Vocation and Lifelong Commitment* (Collegeville, Minn.: The Liturgical Press, 1992) 56–69; Nemeck and Coombs, *The Way of Spiritual Direction* (1985) 15–32; Nemeck and Coombs, *Contemplation* (1982) 13–20.

10. *Life*, 8, 5. See *Catechism*, CCC 2709.

11. *Life*, 13, 22.

12. For some works on the general development of spirituality see: Jordan Aumann, O.P., Thomas Hopko and Donald G. Bloesch, *Christian Spirituality East & West* (Chicago: Priory, 1968); Louis Bouyer, Oratorian, *History of Christian Spirituality*, I, II, III (New York: Seabury, 1963); Louis Dupré and Don E. Saliers, eds., *Christian Spirituality*, I, II, III (New York: Crossroad, 1989); Michael Cox, *Handbook of Christian Spirituality* (San Francisco: Harper & Row, 1985); Jean Gautier, *Some Schools of Catholic Spirituality* (New York: Desclée, 1959); Evelyn Underhill, *Mystics of the Church* (Cambridge, England: Clarke, 1975).

For some works on prayer in the Bible see: Gerhard Kittel and Gerhard Friedrich, eds., *Theological Dictionary of the New Testament*, II (Grand Rapids, Mich.: Eerdmans, 1964) 775–808; or the abridged one-volume edition (1985) 279–285; Thomas Corbishley, S.J., *The Prayer of Jesus* (Garden City, N.Y.: Doubleday, 1977); A. Hamman, *Prayer: The New Testament* (Chicago: Franciscan Herald Press, 1971); Paul Hilsdale, ed., *Prayers from St. Paul* (New York: Sheed & Ward, 1964); Jules Lebreton, S.J., *The Spiritual Teaching of the New Testament* (Westminister, Md.: Newman, 1960) 216–229; Herbert Lockyer, *All the Prayers of the Bible* (Grand Rapids, Mich.: Zondervan, 1959); David M. Stanley, S.J., *Boasting in the Lord: The Phenomenon of Prayer in Saint Paul* (New York: Paulist, 1973); Gordon P. Wiles, *Paul's Intercessory Prayers* (New York: Cambridge University Press, 1974).

For some works on prayer in Christian antiquity see: Louis Bouyer, Oratorian, *The Spirituality of the New Testament and the Fathers* (New York: Seabury, 1960) 256–522; F. Forrester Church and Terrence J. Mulry, eds. *Earliest Christian Meditations* (New York: Macmillan, 1989); Thomas A. Hand, O.S.A, *St. Augustine on Prayer* (Dublin: M.H. Gill, 1963); Bernard McGinn, *The Foundations of Mysticism: Origins to the Fifth Century* (New York: Crossroad, 1991); Hugh Pope, O.P., *The Teaching of St. Augustine on Prayer and the Contemplative Life* (London, England: Burns & Oates, 1935).

For some works on prayer from the Middle Ages to modern times see: Josef A. Jungmann, *Christian Prayer Through the Centuries* (New York: Paulist, 1978); A Benedictine of Stanbrook Abbey, *Mediaeval Mystical Tradition and Saint John of the Cross* (London, England: Burns & Oates, 1954); Graeme J. Davidson with Mary Macdonald, *Anyone Can*

Pray: A Guide to Methods of Christian Prayer (New York: Paulist, 1983); Giacomo Lercaro, *Methods of Mental Prayer* (London, England: Burns & Oates, 1957); Jane T. Stoddart, *Private Prayer in Christian Story* (London, England: Hodder & Stoughton, 1927).

13. Among the writers who influenced either the theology or the practice of prayer in North America during the first half of the 1900s are: Jordan Aumann, Louis Bouyer, Eugene Boylan, Charles Hugo Doyle, Caryll Houselander, James Keller, Dom Marmion, Robert Nash, Raoul Plus, Alphonsus Rodriguez, Fulton J. Sheen, Adolphe Tanquerey, Evelyn Underhill, Gerald Vann.

Five authors in particular impacted people's understanding and practice of prayer before, during, and immediately after Vatican II: Hans Urs von Balthasar, Louis Evely, Thomas Merton, Karl Rahner, and Pierre Teilhard de Chardin.

Persons who significantly influenced either the theology or the practice of prayer in North America during the second half of the 1900s are: Leonardo Boff, Ruth Burrows, Marie Theresa Coombs, Thomas Dubay, John English, James Finley, Thomas Green, David Hassel, Edward Hays, Thomas Keating, Ernest Larken, John Main, George A. Maloney, Francis Kelly Nemeck, Henri J. M. Nouwen, M. Basil Pennington, Miriam Pollard, David Steindl-Rast, David M. Stanley, Simon Tugwell.

14. See, for example: Kilian McDonnell, *Presence, Power, Praise: Documents on the Charismatic Renewal*, I, II, III (Collegeville, Minn.: The Liturgical Press, 1980); Yves Congar, O.P., *I Believe in the Holy Spirit*, I, II, III (New York: Seabury, 1983); Leonardo Boff, *Ecclesiogenesis: The Base Communities Reinvent the Church* (Maryknoll, N.Y.: Orbis, 1986); Patrick L. Bourgeois, *Can Catholics Be Charismatic?* (Hicksville, N.Y.: Exposition, 1976); Robert Faricy, S.J., and Lucy Rooney, S.N.D., *The Contemplative Way of Prayer* (Ann Arbor, Mich.: Servant, 1986); J. Massyngberde Ford, *Which Way for Catholic Pentecostals?* (New York: Harper & Row, 1976); Brennan Manning, T.O.R., *Prophets and Lovers* (Denville, N.J.: Dimension, 1976).

15. The House of Prayer movement was spearheaded by Margaret Brennan, I.H.M., Ann Chester, I.H.M., Bernard Haring, C.SS.R., and Thomas Merton, O.C.S.O. See: CRUX Publications, ed., *Annual Directory: Houses of Prayer 1979–1980* (Albany, N.Y.: Clarity, 1980).

16. See, for example: James Arraj, *St. John of the Cross and Dr. C.G. Jung* (Chiloquin, Ore.: Tools for Inner Growth, 1986); John Welch, O.Carm, *Spiritual Pilgrims: Carl Jung and Teresa of Avila* (New York: Paulist, 1982); Barbara Metz, S.N.D.N., and John Burchill, O.P., *The Enneagram and Prayer* (Denville, N.J.: Dimension, 1987); Charles J. Keating, *Who We Are Is How we Pray* (Mystic, Conn.: Twenty-Third Publications, 1987); Chester P. Michael and Marie C. Norrisey, *Prayer and Temperament: Different Prayer Forms for Different Personality Types* (Charlottesville, Va.: Open Door, 1984).

17. See, for instance: Matthew Fox, O.P., *Original Blessing* (Santa Fe: Bear, 1983); Frederick Franck, *Zen Seeing, Zen Drawing: Meditation in Action* (New York: Bantam, 1993) and *The Zen of Seeing: Seeing/Drawing as Meditation* (New York: Vintage, 1973); M.C. Richards, *Centering: in Pottery, Poetry and the Person* (Hanover, N.H.: Wesleyan, 1989); Wendy Beckett, *The Mystical Now: Art and the Sacred* (New York: Universe, 1993).

18. Such as Anthony Bloom (Orthodox), Richard J. Foster (Quaker), Morton Kelsey (Episcopalian), Albert C. Outler (Methodist); Maggie Ross (Anglican), Benedicta Ward (Anglican). See: Francois Biot, O.P., *The Rise of Protestant Monasticism* (Baltimore: Helicon, 1963); Louis Bouyer, Oratorian, *Orthodox Spirituality and Protestant and Anglican Spirituality* (New York N.Y.: Seabury, 1969); Frank C. Senn, ed., *Protestant Spiritual Traditions* (Mahwah, N.J.: Paulist, 1986).

19. Among the important contributors in this respect are: Ewert Cousins, Anthony de Mello, Aelred Graham, Bede Griffiths, William Johnston, Philip Kapleau, Raimundo Panikkar, Mary Jo Weaver, Robley Whitson.

20. Contributors to this movement include: Thomas Keating, O.C.S.O.; George A. Maloney, S.J.; M. Basil Pennington, O.C.S.O.; Maggie Ross, Hermit; Benedicta Ward, S.L.G.

21. Contributors to this renewal include: William A. Barry, S.J.; Alexandre Brou, S.J.; John J. English, S.J.; David L. Fleming, S.J.; Josef Neuner, S.J.; Hugo Rahner, S.J.; Juan Luis Segundo, S.J., David M. Stanley, S.J.

22. Contributors to this renewed interest include: James Arraj; Gerald Brenan; Ross Collins, O.C.D.; Marie Theresa Coombs, Hermit; Barbara Dent; Joseph Glynn, O.C.D.; Elizabeth Hamilton; Richard P. Hardy; Kieran Kavanaugh, O.C.D.; Ernest Larkin, O.Carm; Victoria Lincoln; Susan Muto; Francis Kelly Nemeck, O.M.I.; John Sullivan, O.C.D.

23. Contributors to the integration of these elements include: Daniel Berrigan, S.J.; Leonardo Boff; Dom Helder Camara; Ernesto Cardinal; Carlo Carretto; José Comblin; Albert Gelin, S.S.; Gustavo Gutierrez; Dorethee Soelle.

24. The Liturgical Press at St. John's Abbey, Collegeville, Minn., has been in the forefront of the liturgical renewal in North America.

25. Contributors to this ecumenical effort include: Donald Attwater, Jordan Aumann, O.P.: Augustin Bea; Louis Bouyer, C.O.; Ewert H. Cousins; Albert C. Outler; Max Thurian.

26. Contributors to this new appreciation include: Jean Shinoda Bolen, Robert Bly; Joseph Campbell; Sam Keen; Thomas E. Mails; Ed McGaa (Eagle Man); Michael Meade; Robert Moore; Marie-Louise von Franz; Marian Woodman.

27. Contributors to these movements include: Ralph A. DiOrio; Matthew Fox, O.P.; Thomas Berry; Dennis, Sheila, Matthew Linn; Francis MacNutt.

28. Spiritual Directors International has made a major contribution in this area.

29. See, for example: Francis Kelly Nemeck, O.M.I., and Marie Theresa Coombs, Hermit, *O Blessed Night: Recovering from Addiction, Codependency and Attachment based on the Insights of St. John of the Cross and Pierre Teilhard de Chardin* (Staten Island, N.Y.: Alba House, 1991); Gerald G. May, *Addiction and Grace* (San Francisco: Harper & Row, 1988); Flora Slosson Wuellner, *Prayer, Stress, and Our Inner Wounds* (Nashville: Upper Room, 1985).

30. As for periodicals, see for example: *Carmelite Digest* (San Jose, Calif.); *Carmelite Studies* (Washington, D.C.); *Journal of Spiritual Formation* (Pittsburgh, Penn.); *Living Prayer* (Barre, Vt.); *Mystics Quarterly* (Cincinnati); *Spirituality Today* (St. Louis); *Spiritual Life* (Washington, D.C.); *Studia Mystica* (Saratoga Springs, N.Y.); *Studies in the Spirituality of Jesuits* (St. Louis); *Weavings* (Nashville). As for tapes, see for example: *Corpus Video* (Jefferson Valley, N.Y.); *Credence Cassettes* (Kansas City, Mo.); *Don Bosco* (New Rochelle, N.Y.); *Inner Growth* (Chiloquin, Ore.); *Oblate Media* (St. Louis); *Tabor* (Allen, Tex.); *Thinking Allowed* (Berkeley, Calif.); *Weiner* (New Hyde Park, N.Y.); *United States Catholic Conference* (Washington, D.C.).

31. See, for example: William A. Barry, S.J., *Finding God in All Things* (Notre Dame, Ind.: Ave Maria, 1991); Louis Peeters, S.J., *An Ignatian Approach to Divine Union* (Milwaukee: Bruce, 1956); Alexandre Brou, S.J., *Ignatian Methods of Prayer* (Milwaukee: Bruce, 1949) and *The Ignatian Way to God* (1952).

32. See, for example: Francis Kelly Nemeck, O.M.I., and Marie Theresa Coombs, Hermit, *Contemplation* (Collegeville, Minn.: The Liturgical Press, 1982) 36–96 and *The Spiritual Journey* (1987) 75–124; Ruth Burrows, *Ascent to Love*, (Denville, N.J.: Dimension, 1987); St. Paul Carmel, *A Guide to the Stages of Prayer According to St. Teresa of Jesus and St. John of the Cross* (Salamanca, Spain: Gráficas Ortega, 1971); Réginald Garrigou-Lagrange, O.P., *Christian Perfection and Contemplation* (St. Louis: B. Herder, 1937) and *The Three Ages of the Interior Life*, I-II (1948); Barbara Dent, *The Cleansing of the Heart*

(Denville, N.J.: Dimension, 1973); E.W. Trueman Dicken, *The Crucible of Love* (New York: Sheed & Ward, 1963).

33. Especially *The Way of Perfection* and *The Interior Castle* or *The Mansions*.

34. Chapters 8–23. See: Marie-Eugène, O.C.D., *I Want to See God* (Chicago: Fides, 1953) and *I Am a Daughter of the Church* (1955); Madeleine of St. Joseph, O.C.D., *Within the Castle with St. Teresa of Avila* (Chicago: Franciscan Herald Press, 1982); St. Paul Carmel, *A Guide to the Stages of Prayer According to St. Teresa of Jesus and St. John of the Cross* (Salamanca, Spain: Gráficas Ortega, 1971); Vitalis Lehodey, O.C.R., *The Ways of Mental Prayer* (Dublin: M.H. Gill, 1960); Gabriel of St. Mary Magdalen, O.C.D., *St. Teresa of Jesus* (Westminster, Md.: Newman, 1949) and *The Way of Prayer* (Milwaukee: Spiritual Life Press, 1965).

35. See: Francis Kelly Nemeck, O.M.I., and Marie Theresa Coombs, Hermit, *The Spiritual Journey: Critical Thresholds and Stages of Adult Spiritual Genesis* (Collegeville, Minn.: The Liturgical Press, 1987).

36. See: Francis Kelly Nemeck, O.M.I., and Marie Theresa Coombs, Hermit, *Contemplation* (Collegeville, Minn.: The Liturgical Press, 1982) 53–96 and *The Spiritual Journey* (1987) 55–124.

37. See: Joachim Jeremias, *The Prayers of Jesus* (London: SCM Press, 1967); Francis Kelly Nemeck, O.M.I., and Marie Theresa Coombs, Hermit, *Contemplation* (Collegeville, Minn.: Liturgical Press, 1982) 27–35; Leonardo Boff, *The Lord's Prayer: The Prayer of Integral Liberation* (Maryknoll, N.Y.: Orbis, 1979); Thomas Corbishley, S.J., *The Prayer of Jesus* (Garden City, N.Y.: Doubleday, 1966); William J. Doheny, C.S.C., trans. *The Pater Noster of Saint Teresa* (Milwaukee: Bruce, 1942).

SETTING OUT WITH A MAP

There is a story told about a pair of explorers who went off to explore the great river and then returned to their village. The people of the village wanted to know about their exploits and so the explorers tried to share with them the great expanse of the river, its depth and majesty. They told the villagers about the animals that lived along the river and the fish that inhabited the great waterway. They spoke in detail about the swift currents and the calm pools. The more they told, the more the villagers wanted to hear. Finally the explorers said to themselves, "We will draw them a map of the great river so the villagers can travel it themselves and experience for themselves the magnificence and mystery that we experienced and can only partially convey." So they carefully drew them a map.

The villagers leaped on the map: they had it enlarged, made copies for their homes, and had the original framed and hung in the town hall. And they were sure that they now knew the river. "After all," the villagers said. "Don't we know its every turn and eddy, and can't we list by heart the names of the animals that wander its shore and the fish that swim in its water." They even had fights over who had interpreted the map most clearly, and who knew it most completely.

The explorers only shook their heads. Making the map had been a big mistake, for the people had replaced the experience of the river with knowledge of the map.*

In concluding this text on the *Catechism of the Catholic Church,* we return to some of the questions asked in the first chapter. How does our understanding of catechesis shape the way in which we read the *Catechism?* What is the role of the *Catechism* in contemporary catechesis? One way to speak about the *Catechism* is in terms of the image of a map. The *Catechism* can serve as a map: a map that points the way and helps us to name the experience of the mystery of God's love.

The villagers were mistaken: knowing the map is not knowing the river. But, with map in hand and reflecting on the experience of those who have gone before them, the villagers can set off on their own journey. The map does make navigating the river easier. And from their own experience, the villagers can nuance the map, make clearer the markings, and then pass it on to the next generation.

The image of the *Catechism* as a map has a number of helpful implications for our understanding of its role in faith formation. First, as a map, the *Catechism* situates our journey of faith within the context of those who have gone before us. The long tradition of those who have known the mystery of God's love and have struggled to put that into words are expressed for us today in the *Catechism*. While each generation, each group of believers must take the journey of faith for themselves, the text provides some clear markings to set out the right path. The *Catechism* also gives some clear boundaries about who God is, who Jesus is, and who human beings are. We cross these boundaries only at risk and for very good reason.

Second, as a map, the *Catechism* sets out a shared image around which to plan journeys as individuals and as communities of faith. No generation of believers begins from scratch as they attempt to express who they are through community, liturgy, teaching, and service. A commonly held understanding of what we believe, how we worship, how we are to act, and how we are to pray gives unity to the diverse journeys of faith that come together within the Roman Catholic Church.

Third, as a map, the *Catechism* serves as an important reference tool for later maps. Our own journeys of faith — as individuals, as communities of faith, as a universal Church — will push at the *Catechism*'s boundaries. Our journeys of faith will go into regions to which this map has no reference. We will re-think and re-explore regions that the writers of the *Catechism* think are settled. As we continue to live out of and reflect upon the theology that underpins and flows from the Second Vatican Council, we must continually return to the text of the *Catechism* to change it, clarify it, make it more readable, and more usable for the next generation. Eventually, then, we will have to come up with a new text, building on this one perhaps, but looking very different as well. The *Catechism* itself makes clear the limits of formulas and the role of maps:

> We do not believe in formulas, but in those realities they express, which faith allows us to touch. "The believer's act [of faith] does not terminate in the propositions, but in the realities [which they express]." All the same, we do approach these realities with the help of formulations of the faith which permit us to express the faith and to hand it on, to celebrate it in community, to assimilate and live on it more and more (CCC 170).

The role of the catechist and of all involved in formation is to be map-readers *extraordinaires,* and equally important, to teach others to read the map, to learn the way, and to recognize his or her own life's journey within the vision set out here. In doing so, we help to build up the cartographers of the future, those who will continue to reflect upon our experience, to examine the tradition with believing yet critical eyes, in the hope to ever more closely approximate the mystery of God.

*A version of this story appears in Anthony de Mello, *The Song of the Bird* (New York: Doubleday, 1984) 32–33.

CONTRIBUTORS

TIMOTHY BACKOUS, O.S.B., has been a Benedictine monk of St. John's Abbey since 1979. During that time he has taught English at St. John's Preparatory School, served as Chair of the Preparatory School's English department, and worked with the ESL program. After completing his doctoral studies at the Alphonsianum in 1989, Father Timothy returned from Rome to teach moral theology in the college and graduate school at St. John's. Currently, he serves as chaplain of the university. Besides his class work, Father Timothy also gives frequent talks and workshops in the local area and around the country.

MARIE THERESA COOMBS lives as a canonically recognized hermit at Lebh Shomea, a contemplative-eremitical house of prayer in the desert of South Texas. She earned a masters degree in theological studies from Oblate School of Theology, San Antonio, Texas. Currently, she is pursuing doctoral studies at Graduate Theological Foundation in Donaldson, Indiana. Besides coauthoring several books on prayer and spirituality, she is a frequented spiritual director.

MICHAEL P. HORAN teaches religious education in the Department of Theological Studies at Loyola Marymount University, Los Angeles, California, where he directs the M.A. program in Pastoral Studies. Horan holds a Ph.D. in religious education from The Catholic University of America. His pastoral experience includes youth ministry and leadership formation among college students at Catholic University of America and Iona College, New Rochelle, New York, he has also contributed to catechist formation in the archdiocese of New York.

FRANCIS KELLY NEMECK has been a Missionary Oblate of Mary Immaculate since 1955 and a priest since 1961. He has taught theology in the United States and Canada, besides having missionary and pastoral experience in Texas and Mexico. He earned a masters degree in religious education from the University of Ottawa in Canada and holds a doctorate in spirituality from Les Facultés Catholiques de Lyon in France. Since 1974, he has served as director of Lebh Shomea, has authored and coauthored several books, and is a frequented spiritual director.

JANE E. REGAN is a member of the faculty of the School of Theology at St. John's University in Collegeville, teaching in the area of pastoral theology. Her academic background — a doctorate in catechetics from The Catholic University —

sity of America — is complemented by her pastoral experience. She has worked in religious education on parish and diocesan levels and presently serves as a consultant to her parish's faith formation program. She regularly facilitates workshops on leadership formation and alternative models for catechesis throughout the Midwest.

INDEX

Augustine, *Enchiridion* 25, 26–27

Beatitude 123

Catechetical directory 40–42, 57
Catechesis
  as set out in *Catechism* 7, 19–20
  community as agent 17–19
  historical development 14–19
  Synod of 1985 47–50
Catechism of the Catholic Church
  development of 63–65
  language in 65–66
  structure 66–69
  In Brief sections 68–69, 113
Catechisms
  comparison of large and small
    33–34
  of Claude Fleury 36–37
  of Council of Trent 34–35
  of Martin Luther 31–32
  of Peter Canisius 32–33
  of the Third Council of Baltimore
    39–40
  proposed at Vatican Council I
    38–39
Christology
  as set out in *Catechism* 79–85
  ascending 82–85
  descending 80–82
  Judaism and 82–83
  reign of God and 83–84
Church 86–90
Common good 120, 122, 126–127
Commandments 128–129

Conscience 124–125
Constitution on the Sacred Liturgy
  99–101
Contemplation 141–142, 148, 149

Dei Filius 74–75, 77
Dei Verbum 72–74

Eucharist 109 110
Elucidarium 29

Faith 76–77

Gaudium et Spes 86, 120–121, 132
Grace 104–107, 113, 123
Gerson, Jean 30
Gregory of Nyssa, *Catechetical
  Instruction* 25–26

Hofinger, Johannes 16–17
Holy Spirit 85–86

Ignatius of Loyola 148

John of the Cross 148–150
Jungmann, Josef 14–16

Kerygmatic movement 16

Liturgical catechesis 106, 110–111
Liturgy
  as set out in *Catechism* 97–99
  paschal mystery 98–99, 101, 110
  trinitarian 97–98
  diversity and 108, 113
  catechesis and 106, 110–111

Lord's Prayer   154–159
Lumen Gentium   86, 88, 143

Meditation   141–142, 148
Ministry   89

Paschal mystery   16, 98–99
Pecham, John, "On the Instruction
   of Simple Folk"   28
Prayer
   Catechism approach to   138–142
   progress in prayer   147–154
   twentieth-century renewal
      144–147
   universal call to holiness   142–144

Revelation   71–78

scripture and tradition   74–76
   Dei Verbum   72–73
   Dei Filius   74–75

Sacraments   101–104, 107–109
   as community events 101–102,
      106, 107, 111–112
Sin   122–123
Social justice   125–126
Synod of 1985
   on catechesis   47–50
   on collegiality   52–53
   on inculturation   50–52, 58
   proposed catechism   1, 23, 44–47

Teresa of Jesus   143–144, 150–151